You Are Not a Sh*tty Parent

How to Practice SELF-COMPASSION and Give Yourself a Break

CARLA NAUMBURG, PhD

WORKMAN PUBLISHING • NEW YORK

For Daniela, you're my favorite. I love you.

Library of Congress Cataloging-in-Publication Data is available.

ISBN 978-1-5235-1711-4

Design by Sarah Smith

Workman books are available at special discounts when purchased in bulk for premiums and sales promotions as well as for fundraising or educational use. Special editions or book excerpts can also be created to specification. For details, please contact the Special Sales Director at specialmarkets@workman.com.

Workman Publishing Co., Inc.
225 Varick Street
New York, NY 10014 -4381
workman.com

Printed in the USA on responsibly sourced paper.
First printing August 2022

10 9 8 7 6 5 4 3 2 1

Contents

INTRODUCTION

Why I Wrote a Whole Damn Book About Self-Compassion

Not long after the world shut down in the spring of 2020, I started getting phone calls from journalists and podcasters who wanted to interview me about my book, *How to Stop Losing Your Sh*t with Your Kids*. After weeks, and then months, of trying to balance homeschooling with working from home with the anxiety of living through a pandemic with the stress of not even having two minutes to pee in privacy, parents were absolutely losing their shit with their kids.

Of course they were. We all were.

And so I got on those calls and I talked about parental shit loss and offered suggestions as often and as helpfully as I could. And almost every interview ended with the same question: "If you could leave parents with just one idea or practice or piece of advice, what would it be?"

That was often my favorite part of the conversation because it finally gave me a chance to dive into the topic I really wanted to talk about: self-compassion. Interviewers rarely asked about compassion because, well, it's kind of weird. It seems all loosey-goosey and touchy-feely and when the shit is hitting the fan and it feels like the entire world is falling apart, we parents don't need some feel-good baloney. We need answers. We need strategies and solutions.

Or so we think.

But here's the thing that most folks don't realize: Self-compassion *is* the strategy that will help us find the solution, or at least the best way through the storm.

Sometimes, if we're lucky, we can find a fix to whatever's going on. If that's the case, jump on it and do a little happy dance because those moments don't come along as often as we've been led to believe. More often than not, though, much of what we're struggling with either a) isn't a "you" or "your family" problem at all; it's a communal or societal issue that you can't fix on your own, no matter how hard you try, or b) isn't fixable at all, on any level, in which case all we can do is muddle through as best we can.

I knew all of this, but I also knew that a thirty-minute parenting podcast wasn't the time or place to get on my tiny little soapbox and start ranting about the lack of childcare and health care and mental health treatment and support that every single one of us needs—even when it's not a freaking pandemic. Instead, I talked about why we lose it and the importance of sleep and singletasking and moving our bodies in helping us stay calm. While I'm sure some of this advice was useful, I also worried that every time I suggested something parents should be doing differently, I was implying that if parents were struggling, it was because they were doing something wrong.

And that couldn't be further from the truth.

I'm not saying that parents couldn't be doing better; we all could, because that's the deal with being a human parent raising human kids. I'm just saying that in that moment, telling parents to try to take care of themselves so they could be calmer and more flexible in the face of COVID chaos was kind of like blaming parents for a gaping wound they didn't cause and then getting all hung up on which shape Band-Aid they should be using and how often they should be changing it. Certainly, when Band-Aids are all you've got, of course you're going to focus on them and that's fine. But we sure as shit shouldn't be blaming ourselves when they don't solve the fundamental problem.

And that's what I saw parents doing again and again: blaming themselves for not fixing the unfixable problems of life and parenting. For not staying calm at every moment. For not doing a better job managing their children's online learning. For leaving their jobs and stalling out their careers in order to care for the kids or for not leaving their jobs and not having enough time or energy for their families. For not making their kids get more exercise or letting them have too much screen time. For eating too much, drinking too much, buying too much crap online, and being just too damn fried and overwhelmed to even get through the day, much less parent, the way they wanted to.

And these aren't just pandemic problems; these are challenges parents have faced since the beginning of time. The pandemic was just another endless, relentless straw that broke the already overburdened camel's back.

Which is why I kept talking about self-compassion. There was no way I was ending the conversation with yet another piece of "should" advice. I wanted to give listeners the antidote to the isolation, judgment, and self-contempt that I knew far too many parents had been experiencing for years and were now buried in. And so I seized my moment and started spreading the news about connection and curiosity and kindness as often as I could to as many people as I could. I like to think it helped just a little.

Even if it did, things still got worse for parents. As the world started opening up again in the fall of 2021, we began to get data confirming what we already knew: that kids had suffered academically, mentally, emotionally, physically, and socially during the yearlong lockdown. Even though parents had been forced to choose between Shitty and Even Shittier, they blamed themselves for their children's struggles. They compared their own unwinnable situations to those of parents with more money, more resources, flexible jobs, better school systems, and access to childcare and health care and wondered why they didn't measure up.

Feeling like shitty parents isn't just another side effect of this damn pandemic (although it's a bad one); somehow it has become the theme song of our generation. For a variety of reasons we'll discuss, we parents have been holding ourselves to impossible standards, blaming ourselves for situations beyond our control, and treating ourselves like shit when we screw up.

We're suffering from Shitty Parent Syndrome, which I define as the thought, belief, or perception that you are a shitty parent, when, in fact, you're not. Shitty Parent Syndrome looks a little different for everyone, but generally speaking, it consists of three different reactions we tend to have when things fall apart or we feel like we're failing: isolation, judgment, and contempt.

We assume we're the only ones who have ever suffered and screwed up the way we're suffering and screwing up, we judge the shit out of ourselves for it, and we treat ourselves as if we don't deserve even the most basic approval or respect.

And here's the bitch of it all: Believing you're a shitty parent and treating yourself that way doesn't make anything better.

No one functions well when they feel completely worthless. I know from experience.

I spent my early parenting years neck-deep in Shitty Parent Syndrome. I wasn't just judging myself each time I lost my shit with my kids or reacted poorly to a situation; I was also completely convinced that I was a terrible mom because I despised playing dolls with my girls and I wasn't making home-cooked meals every single night and potty training was beyond a nightmare and they never seemed to have the right shoes and my part-time work schedule meant I wasn't spending enough time with my kids and even when I was, I wasn't calm or patient or

Where did Shitty Parent Syndrome come from? We'll dive into this in Chapter 5, but for now what you need to know is that it has nothing to do with the quality of your parenting. We can—and will—epically screw up, and that doesn't mean we're shitty parents. It just means we're humans doing the hardest job any of us will ever do. Our tendencies toward isolation, judgment, and self-contempt arise from a toxic combination of too much advice, too little support, and the inevitable comparisons that arise in the face of social media and (un)reality television. What I hope you can keep in mind is that no matter how specific and personal your shitty parent thoughts and beliefs may seem, they have very little to do with the quality of your parenting and a whole lot to do with how we've all been trained to judge the crap out of ourselves.

happy enough—whether we were playing Candy Land for the first time or fifty-seventh time that week.

I thought I was a terrible mom because raising kids was really, really hard and I never felt like I was doing it as well or enjoying it as much as everyone else seemed to be.

Not only did my Shitty Parent Syndrome feel like crap, but it made everything so much harder. It's not like all that time I spent hiding in the pantry and eating chocolate chips straight out of the bag calmed me down or helped me think more clearly or creatively about whatever was going on. And you and I both know that comparing myself to all those other parents out there—the ones who seemed so damn perfect—didn't do shit for my confidence. I felt exhausted, defeated, doubtful, anxious, and confused, and there's no scenario in which that helped me be more patient and present with my kids.

But I didn't realize any of that at the time. I had no idea how harmful my self-shame and self-blame was, so I kept hustling. I was certain that if I could just *do* better, if I could just find the right advice and follow it well enough and make the right choices and respond the right way, I wouldn't be a shitty parent anymore. And if I wasn't actually a shitty parent, then I wouldn't feel like one, right?

Yeah, well, not so much.

Because here's the thing. Sure, I was losing my shit with my kids and feeding them boxed mac 'n' cheese for dinner and refusing to play princess and putting them in front of the TV when I should have been finger painting.

But I wasn't a shitty parent.

And neither are you.

If you're not a shitty parent, does that mean you're a good one? Woof. That's the big question, isn't it? Are we good parents? What makes a good parent? I have spent years—YEARS, I tell you!—struggling with this issue and I can tell you with great confidence that *I have no freaking clue*. There are as many ways to raise our children well as there are families on this planet, and even if we get it all right (whatever the hell that means), there's still no guarantee that everything's going to work out well (again, whatever the hell that means). But I do know one thing with absolute certainty: Believing the shitty parent story that's kicking around in your brain isn't going to get you any closer to being a great parent, whatever that looks like for you and your family.

But What If You Actually Are a Shitty Parent?

Chances are some version of this question is hanging out somewhere in the back of your mind, because you picked up this book. Even though I don't believe there's such a thing as shitty parents, my guess is that you don't yet feel the same way. And if we don't talk about it (by which I mean, me writing at you about it), then it's always going to be there, nagging at you, undermining you at every turn.

Most parents suffering from Shitty Parent Syndrome behave in one or more of the following ways:

1. You blame yourself for choices and situations that aren't really a problem. Maybe you don't have the time or energy or money to make your daughter play a sport or take advanced math tutoring, or you're not raising them to be bilingual. Or your full-time job means your kids have to stay in afterschool and you can't make it to every game. Or you don't really enjoy being with kids, and you feel guilty for how often you wish you were alone on a beach or roaming the aisles of Target or even just sitting in the back of your closet if that's what it would take for the love of god. Or you feel like you should be doing a better job making your kids happy, and you have no idea how to do that.

While these are very real experiences and concerns, let's get crystal clear about one thing: None of these are examples of bad parenting. They're just moments when your reality doesn't measure up to the BS fantasy our society has created about how parenting should look. Shoot, we might as well judge ourselves for not having a petting zoo in the backyard because that's about as realistic.

2. You blame yourself for habits and reactions that fall somewhere between "less than ideal" and "moderately screwed up" (which, in clinical terms, we would call "normal"). I'm talking about exploding at or disconnecting from your family more often than you're comfortable with, forgetting to send your kiddo with a lunch, not following through on promises, lying to your kids because you have no freaking clue how to tell them the truth, not setting limits, not listening when they need you to, etc. etc. (I'll stop there because I know your brain is already off and running with your own List of Reasons Why You Suck and that's totally not the vibe we're going for here.)

Unless I'm wrong (which I'm not), you skipped right past the whole "normal" part I just mentioned and dove headfirst into the List of Reasons Why You Suck. Please don't do that. Instead, try to remember that a) perfection can suck it and b) our kids don't need us to be perfect. They just need us to live our lives as best we can, love them as best we can, and show them—through our words and actions—that it's OK to get confused and make mistakes and feel bad and none of it makes us bad kids or bad parents.

3. Sometimes you cross the line. Hitting your kids. Repeatedly saying cruel, hurtful, abusive things to them. Drinking or using drugs to the point that it's interfering with your ability to show up for your kids and take care of them. When that's the case, it doesn't mean that you're a shitty parent or a shitty person. It just means you don't have the information, support, and resources to do better right now. Chances are you already feel alone, ashamed, and confused as hell. You don't need to pile on a load of judgment and contempt on top of that, and that's exactly what all your Shitty Parent Thoughts are doing. What you need are folks who can hear your stories, get curious about your experience, and treat you with kindness as they help you heal, change, and become the kind of parent you want to be. And while a book might be total crap at listening to you, reading this one is a powerful first step on the journey toward finding those people.

Regardless of how many of those boxes you check in these three scenarios, regardless of the details of your situation, regardless of how severe your Shitty Parent Syndrome is, let me say it loud and clear: You are not a shitty parent.

I'm going to say that again, this time in italics, to make sure you don't miss it. *You are not a shitty parent.*

Not to get all shouty at you, but I'm going to write it in capital letters because this is really important. YOU ARE NOT A SHITTY PARENT.

Shoot. I'm not just saying it. I wrote a whole damn book about it.

This is the part where some of you are thinking, yeah, OK, but what about the Super-Duper Shitty Parents out there? The ones who are horribly abusive and neglectful and legitimately suck at parenting? This is an important point, because there are absolutely folks who make terrible parenting choices and treat their children really badly. But I will never, ever call them Shitty Parents. My goal—as a clinical social worker, mother, and person on this planet—is to help folks grow and heal and become more engaged, empathic, and effective parents. And telling someone they're a Shitty Parent is never, ever going to achieve that. So, yes, there are parents out there who need a huge amount of help and support, but maybe instead of labeling them, we can get curious about what they need, or at the very least, offer them a whole lot of compassion?

Why I Wrote a Whole Damn Book About Why You're Not a Shitty Parent

At some point, I realized that spending three minutes on self-compassion at the end of every podcast interview wasn't enough. I might be able to introduce the idea, but parents need so much more than a sound bite. We need the skills and strategies that will help us get past the shame and self-contempt that leave us feeling stuck, confused, and doubtful of our decisions and ability to parent well. When we can respond to the shittiest moments of parenting with compassion rather than contempt, we feel calmer, think more clearly, and respond more creatively and confidently to whatever's going on.

Let me give you an example.

Imagine you're on a hike with your kids. You had set out for an easy walk through the woods, but somewhere along the way, you took a wrong turn and now you have no idea where you are. The kids are getting hungry and cranky, and you're not doing much better yourself. Maybe your back is aching or your knee is acting up, but either way, you're definitely starting to feel anxious. You need to get your family back to the car before things get really bad.

To top it all off, your partner is giving you shit about not downloading the map onto your phone before you set out on this godforsaken hike. Maybe they wanted to go mini-golfing instead and they're taking every opportunity to remind you that nobody—not a single person in the entire history of the universe—has ever gotten lost on a mini-golf course. Thanks for that one, babe.

And now one of the kids has fallen and scraped her knee and she's crying and the other one needs to poop and you didn't bring whatever the hell one is supposed to bring into the woods to deal with poop because this wasn't even supposed to be a hike, it was just supposed to be a walk, and how the hell did you screw this up so badly?

Ugh.

Just when you're about to give up and let your child poop in the woods, you see a ranger coming down the trail. Yay! You're saved! As you explain your situation, the ranger reaches into her bag and hands you a map. Hallelujah! The nightmare is over, and you'll be back in the car before everything goes to shit, literally and figuratively.

You thank the ranger, and she heads on her way. But as you unfold the paper, you realize there are no squiggly lines representing trails. There are no clear markers for getting back to your car. There are only these words: YOU'RE LOST.

You scan down the page and keep reading.

YOU'RE THE ONLY ONE WHO'S LOST.

YOU SUCK.

PS: YOU'RE A SHITTY PARENT.

Maybe at that moment, another family goes marching past you, happy as freaking clams, clearly knowing where they're going, smiling and singing as if they just walked off the set of *The Sound of Music.*

No way in hell you're going to ask them for directions.

Try to imagine how you might feel in such a moment: anxious, scared, overwhelmed, confused, ashamed, irritable, and maybe just a little pissed at that jerk of a ranger who gave you such a useless map. And I'm guessing that you'd feel alone on a beach or roaming the aisles of Target or even just sitting in the back of your closet, frustrated with yourself for getting your family lost in the first place. Perhaps you can't stop thinking about what a pathetic idiot you are, and how a better parent wouldn't have made such a moronic mistake, as evidenced by Captain von Trapp and his crew of obnoxiously happy campers. Chances are good you'd end up feeling super defensive and snapping at your family. You'd almost certainly have a hard time staying calm, thinking clearly and creatively, and feeling confident in your ability to get your family home safely.

So that sucks.

Fortunately, this is a book, not reality, which means we can go back and rewrite this story. Let's imagine that when the ranger showed up, she gave you a different map, another one without any trails or markers. But it did have these words:

YOU'RE LOST.

IT'S OK. EVERYONE GETS LOST SOMETIMES.

HANG IN THERE. YOU'LL FIGURE THIS OUT.

PS: YOU'RE AN AWESOME PARENT.

At first glance, this map might not seem much better than the first one. It doesn't tell you which trail to follow or how to get back to your car, but it does point you in the direction of self-compassion. And my guess is that you'll feel way less stressed and overwhelmed after reading it. You might even feel comfortable asking the happy hiker family for directions. Or maybe your head will get clear enough for you to remember that you have some tissues and a plastic bag in the bottom of your backpack, so you can help your kiddo poop and at least get that taken care of. Maybe you recall a game your grandfather used to play with you every time you went on a hike with him, and that helps distract the kids while you figure out what to do.

Even though you don't have a perfect answer for what to do next, the whole situation feels a little easier and more manageable. And when you consider how frequently we parents feel lost, that's not nothing.

Unfortunately, there's no parenting paradise where we don't get lost sometimes. There's no version of raising kids where we don't make mistakes or react poorly or lose our shit or feel terrible. There's no scenario where we or our children escape the epic fails, broken friendships, brutal diagnoses, lost loved ones, and general pain of living a life.

That's the bad news.

Thankfully for all of us mortal humans, there's also good news. Really good news. No matter how hard things get, no matter how lost you feel, no matter how convinced you are that you are absolutely and completely unequipped to deal with any of this, you always have that second map with you. You can pull it out any time you find yourself out in the middle of the woods with cranky kids and a grumpy partner and no freaking clue which way to turn. You can pull it out anytime you feel like the shittiest parent in the history of the universe. Compassion may not tell you where to go or how to solve all your problems, but it will help you stay calm, think clearly and creatively, and give you the confidence to take the next step for yourself and your family.

And even better—it's free and available to every single parent, every single person on the planet, regardless of your culture, community, religious beliefs, family structure, socioeconomic status, or any other factor in your life. It's a simple yet powerful strategy, especially for those of us who are stuck in a habit of shame and blame. Learning to respond to yourself with understanding, forgiveness, and acceptance requires practice, but it's 100 percent worth it.

Look, I've been on a lot of shitty hikes in my life, and I know I'll be on a lot more. Learning to put down my crap map and pick up the maps of compassion has changed my life and my parenting.

Self-Compassion Isn't Just a Nice Idea—It's an Active Choice

Most folks who aren't social work nerds tend to clump words like "compassion" and "sympathy" and "empathy" and "unicorns farting glitter rainbows" together. It's all hippie-dippie drum-circle kumbaya nonsense that sounds nice enough but has nothing to do with the reality of your lives, with the overdue bills and cranky in-laws and that weird-ass rash on your kid's arm that you were kind of hoping would go away if you just ignored it but it's still there and the only pediatric dermatologist in network is an hour away.

Don't get me wrong; I love sympathy and empathy and unicorns farting glitter rainbows as much as the next gal, but compassion isn't just how you think or feel about whatever's going on. It's a completely different animal (so to speak). Compassion is more like a unicorn who shows up every time you're really struggling and reminds you that you're not alone, gets curious about what's going on, listens to what you need, and responds with kindness. The unicorn doesn't offer any parenting advice, because, well, unicorns don't know shit about human kids, but somehow their mere presence makes you feel so much better that you forgive them for all the glitter they left behind.

The point here is that self-compassion isn't just about *noticing* when you are suffering (although the noticing is such a big deal that we're going to spend an entire chapter on it), it's also about *taking action* in response to our suffering, both in the ways we choose to think about whatever is going on and how we treat ourselves. In fact, the action part is so crucial that I briefly considered combining compassion + action into a new word. Compaction. But then I remembered some fairly painful prune juice–related moments when my daughters were in diapers, so I'm gonna steer clear of that the whole compaction thing.

Hopefully you still get the point.

How This Book Works

We'll start by exploring why we treat ourselves so poorly, why that's so problematic for our parenting, and how, exactly, self-compassion makes everything so much easier and more manageable. From there, we'll dive into four very specific and surprisingly powerful practices of self-compassion—noticing, connection, curiosity, and kindness—that will counteract the

Shitty Parent Syndrome tendencies of isolation, judgment, and contempt and help you respond to even the roughest parenting moments in the most effective and empathic ways possible. We'll talk about how to integrate each of these into your life and parenting, and how they'll benefit your children, both directly and indirectly.

First up, *connection*. One of the most insidious aspects of Shitty Parent Syndrome is the belief that we're the only parents who didn't sign their kids up for flute lessons or aren't sure how to handle a meltdown in aisle three or don't know when to be worried that our first grader isn't reading yet. We think we're the only ones who have rage fits and escape fantasies. All those isolating thoughts aren't just complete and total bullshit, but they're also self-perpetuating because the more alone we think we are, the less likely we are to reach out for support when we need it the most. Learning to recognize those thoughts and choosing to respond by connecting—to the present moment, common humanity, and trusted adults—can go a long way toward helping us get a new perspective on our parenting.

From there, we can get *curious* about our experience, about what's really happening in our lives, our families, our bodies and minds, and how we're thinking, feeling, and behaving in response. So often we jump straight to judgment, which leads to irritability, confusion, and obsessive fixing behaviors. Rarely do we slow down and notice what's going on, how much of it we actually have control over, and what we really need in order to deal with everything as well as possible. As we'll explore more, curiosity is an inherently compassionate response, and it's often an incredibly useful source of important information.

No matter what's going on, we can always respond to ourselves with *kindness*. Kindness may seem straightforward, but it often gets confused and tangled up with all sorts of issues around discipline, limit setting, and personal responsibility. Kindness isn't necessarily about being nice, and it's not always about making yourself or others feel better (although that can be a pleasant side effect!). Kindness is not blaming ourselves for your child's dyslexia diagnosis. Kindness is letting go of that internal voice that keeps berating you for working when you should be parenting or parenting when you should be working. Kindness is noticing when you're completely depleted and choosing to say no to the latest volunteer request rather than judging ourselves for not being more on top of our shit. When you can get clear on what it means to be kind, what it doesn't, and what kindness actually looks like in your daily lives, you develop an entirely new and surprisingly effective strategy, one that makes parenting easier and way more fun.

Those of you who read my previous book, *How to Stop Losing Your Sh*t with Your Kids*, may notice a few similarities between these two books. First, good on you for remembering something you read! Secondly, you're right, and that's because self-compassion is a powerful strategy for not losing your shit. It's also a super effective and empathic way to respond to the challenges of parenting and life in general.

But wait! There's more! Your compassion practice will benefit your children in a variety of different ways, whether or not you ever tell them what you're doing. Each time you respond to painful, challenging, or confusing moments with connection, curiosity, and kindness, you'll not only decrease the stress and tension in the house, but you'll be modeling a more skillful way to deal with the tough stuff of life. In addition, you can explicitly teach these strategies to your children, and we'll talk more about that in Chapter 8. But you don't need to worry about that now. Your compassion practice starts with you, so let's dig in.

CHAPTER ONE

Crap Happens and Then We Make It Worse

Let's go back to that ill-fated hike from the previous chapter. Thanks to that helpful second map, you managed to make your way back to the car with relatively little drama. You're feeling good about your recovery, and you want to find as many opportunities as possible to get your family outside and off their screens. So you plan another hike. You plan a failproof hike.

You drag a grumbling, cranky family out the door and proudly show them the sign at the trailhead, which reads:

THIS IS AN EXTREMELY SAFE AND EASY TRAIL. NO ONE HAS EVER GOTTEN INJURED, LOST, OR EVEN THE LEAST BIT CONFUSED OR UNHAPPY ON THIS HIKE SINCE THIS TRAIL WAS FIRST CREATED. ENJOY YOUR DAY!

The sun is out, the sky is blue, and it's not long before everyone is in a good mood. Shoot, you're so happy that you don't even get annoyed at your daughter's endless story about the latest third-grade playground drama.

And that's when the arrows start flying.

Literal, actual arrows.

They come out of nowhere and before you can even figure out what the hell is going on, you take one in the side. OUCH. That shit stings.

And then you freak out. Of course you do, because who wouldn't lose their freaking shit if they got struck by a freaking arrow while they were on what was supposed to be the safest freaking hike in the history of hikes? It's not like you took your family for a walk through an archery range, for Pete's sake. And so you panic and your heart starts racing and you can't breathe and it's not just because you've got an arrow in your side. This wasn't supposed to happen. What did you do wrong? And how the hell are you the only parent on the planet who can't take your kids on even one successful hike?

So there you are, on the side of the trail, writhing in pain and self-doubt while your partner gets going about how nobody in the history of the universe has ever been struck by an arrow on a mini-golf course and your son starts blathering on about these amazing arrows he made in Minecraft once and your daughter starts wondering if this is an intruder drill like the ones she practiced at school, which of course triggers the shit out of you, but you still have a damn arrow in your side and it really freaking hurts and you're starting to wonder if you should try to pull it out or if this is one of those situations you only see on TV where you're supposed to leave it in so you don't start spurting blood everywhere and you're not sure if this is something you actually want to google or not.

You're just about to pull out your phone when a paramedic comes hiking up the trail. HURRAH! You're saved! He immediately removes the arrow, but instead of bandaging you up, he reaches into his bag, pulls out another arrow, and jams it straight into the open wound.

What. The. Actual. Fuck.

This Ridiculous Story Is a Metaphor for Parenting

This ridiculous story is obviously a metaphor. (Although if for some reason it actually resonates with your hiking experience, then may I humbly suggest you stick to mini-golf?) So let's get into it.

First, that sign at the start of the hike declaring that nothing bad will ever happen. There's a reason you never see signs guaranteeing a perfect experience anywhere. They're not true. They're never true. Even worse, they set unrealistic, unachievable expectations that leave us feeling like shit when we inevitably fail to meet them. And yet from the very moment folks start even thinking about getting pregnant, we're inundated with both subtle and smack-you-across-the-face messages about how parenting should be joyful, intuitive, meaningful, and amazing. Happy isn't just the goal, we're led to believe, it's the norm. It's how everyone else's life is, and how our lives can and should be. And if for some reason they're not, it's because there's something wrong with us or our kids and it's on us to work harder or parent better or find the right specialist or whatever.

Then, of course, there's the arrow. The first arrow, the one that came flying out of nowhere. I wish I could take credit for the arrow idea, but it actually comes from the Buddha (who may have had a young son, which makes his story of running away just so he could hang out alone under a tree for seven weeks fairly relatable). Anyway, the Buddha talked about arrows because, well, guns and reality TV shows and electronic drum sets for kids and all the other things that cause us pain and wreak havoc on our lives hadn't been invented yet. The details don't matter; the point is that that first arrow, the one that seems to come out of nowhere, represents the inevitable chaos, the chronic confusion, disorder, and unpredictability that crashes into our lives, often when we least expect it. These are the fractured arms, ailing parents, cancelled plans, busted refrigerators, empty gas tanks, kids who spike fevers on the days we absolutely have to be at work, problematic texts we probably shouldn't have sent in the first place, unexpected bills we can't cover, school bullies, and global freaking pandemics.

And just like an actual arrow, chaos hurts. Whether it grazes your skin or lodges itself right in your hip, that shit stings. And then we react to that pain because who wouldn't? Unless you're Bruce Willis in *Die Hard*, you're going to freak out in some way when you're in physical or emotional pain; that's just what humans do. And it's not just that these injuries hurt; they also demand our attention, sap our energy and resources, and leave us with terrible scars. Whether we play a role in causing our own chaos or it comes flying in out of nowhere, it complicates our lives and leaves us feeling sad and angry and confused and anxious. To top it all off, it feels extra bad because we've been raised to believe that our lives and our parenting should be calm, cool, and collected, even when we have a freaking arrow hanging out of our hip.

cough bullshit *cough*

Look, I don't care how well you research your hikes or how many (probably fake) guarantees you get or how careful and planful and thoughtful you are, first arrows will fly. That's just what first arrows do. I mean, it sucks, and in some circumstances we might be able to slow them down or soften them a little bit, but make no mistake about it; there's no getting around the first arrows of life.

But that truth doesn't stop us from trying—not because we're hopeless idiots, but because much of the self-help and parenting advice out there is focused on avoiding the first arrows of life—the colicky baby, the job loss, the Celiac diagnosis, the tween who is being bullied at school. And some of that advice works, sometimes, like that clever trick you read online for getting a preschooler to drink that nasty antibiotic. Or the new teen room at the library that actually got your kid to emerge from their bedroom. And even though those first-arrow fixes are like the shittiest game of whack-a-mole ever, we keep at it, because that's what parents do.

One of the most compassionate things we can do for ourselves is not getting sucked into the Big Lie. You know the one I'm talking about—that parenting should be enjoyable and easy, our kids should always be healthy and happy, and we should be in control at all times. But between all that advice and the highly curated and filtered images and situations on social media and reality TV, it's hard not to believe the big lie—that parenting should be enjoyable and easy, our kids should be healthy and happy, and we should be in control.

And so we're left chasing rainbows, with no freaking clue about what to do when the sky opens up and we're left standing in the pouring rain and shouting at the storm. This isn't because there's anything wrong with us; it's just because most of us weren't taught how to deal with the arrows of life. We're told, again and again, that we have to prevent them, but we're given very little insight or information about what to do when the shit hits the fan anyway, as it always will, no matter how hard we hustle. And that's how we become the target for a different arrow, the second arrow of suffering.

The Second Arrow of Suffering

Remember that second arrow? The one that jerk of a paramedic jammed in your side when he should have been bandaging you up? The Buddha referred to that as the second arrow of suffering, and it represents the shame, blame, and contempt we hurl at ourselves every time chaos strikes or we freak out or make a mistake or don't meet our own expectations, or just don't manage everything as perfectly as we've been led to believe we should. Instead of responding to our suffering and pain with kindness, forgiveness, and understanding, we tend to disconnect from our friends and communities, judge ourselves harshly, and treat ourselves with a shitload of contempt.

That second arrow doesn't just hurt, but it also prevents us from healing. Instead of forgiving or bandaging ourselves or getting the support we need or trying to understand what happened in the first place, we end up writhing from the actual pain of the first arrow and the shame and guilt and confusion and anxiety of the second arrow all while trying to reschedule a dentist appointment and figure out why our sister-in-law got pissy on the phone and pick up a barfing kid from school and finish answering a bajillion work emails.

Yeah. Guess whose wound never actually gets taken care of? Guess who's just left wallowing in a bunch of shame and shitty thoughts and feelings?

It's not that we're actively or intentionally ignoring our own needs. It's just that we get hyper-focused on our role in whatever happened, all the ways we think we screwed up or should have responded differently, and all the things that could happen if we don't fix it right away. No matter how painful that first arrow may be, the second one hurts even more because it hits us straight in our soft spot. Our wounded place. In other words, the second arrow takes a universal, totally normal experience and makes it deeply personal. It makes it our fault, our failing.

Ouch.

As the pithy old saying by people who like pithy old sayings goes, "Pain is inevitable, suffering is optional." Even though there's no way to stop those first arrows of life, we can stop blaming and shaming ourselves each time things go poorly or we miss the mark.

But here's the thing: Most of us don't even realize we're shooting ourselves again and again, much less how or why it keeps happening. But we need to get clear on those second arrows if we're going to have a snowball's chance in hell of avoiding them in the future. Here are just a few examples of the second arrows that most of us shoot ourselves with on a daily basis:

We Tell Ourselves We Suck. I'm not talking about accepting responsibility when you make a mistake. That's often a very skillful choice. I'm talking about when our thinking devolves from "Whelp, that was a major snafu" to "I'm a terrible parent and I'm totally screwing up my kids." When we do that, we're judging ourselves and comparing ourselves to others and thinking about all the ways we're getting it wrong and all the ways a better parent would be doing things differently.

Folks suffering from Shitty Parent Syndrome don't even need to pull out our crap maps anymore—we have them memorized. We suck and we know it and everyone knows it and there's nothing we can do about it. We're so skilled at navigating those rocky trails of self-contempt that we can get to the end of the hike, defeated, exhausted, and cranky as hell without a damn clue as to how we got there. And even if we do realize what's happening, we keep following our crap map anyway because a) it's the path of least resistance and we parents are just too damn tired and overwhelmed to blaze a new trail, and b) we don't have any other maps to choose from (at least not yet!).

SNAFU is one of my favorite acronyms; it stands for Situation Normal, All Fucked Up. It originated in the military, but it's made its way into popular lingo. When most folks refer to snafus, they're thinking about the "all fucked up" part, but I prefer to focus on "situation normal" part. Normal, as in typical, usual, or expected. Snafus happen to everyone, and they're no indication that there's anything wrong with us or our parenting.

We Tell Other People We Suck. Everyone loves a good parenting-gone-awry story, and lots of us love telling them. But more often than not, the stories aren't just about the chaos, they're actually about how we caused the chaos and maybe even made it worse and ha ha ha ha guess we won't be winning Parent of the Year anytime soon.

I'm not saying we shouldn't tell these stories of parental mayhem; in fact, just the opposite. As we'll explore more in Chapter 6, connecting authentically with others is a powerful form of self-compassion. The goal is just to make sure we're not throwing ourselves under the bus—no matter how funny it might seem at the time.

We Hang Out with People Who Leave Us Thinking We Suck. Whether we're scrolling through their social media posts or chatting near the swings, the more time we spend with people who don't show up for us in authentic ways and see and accept us for who we are, the harder it is for us to trust and believe in ourselves. When we hang out (either virtually or in real life) with people who present themselves as perfect and their parenting experience as clean and easy and/or judge us for our mega mess, it becomes far too easy to believe that everyone else is nailing this parenting gig and we're the only ones being flattened by it.

We Treat Ourselves Like We Suck. This might be the sneakiest and most insidious of all the second arrows. Every time we put ourselves at the end of the list or minimize our emotional, psychological, and physical needs, we strengthen our underlying beliefs that we're not worthy of care. When we don't reach out for or accept help when we need it, we reinforce the idea that we're alone in how damn hard this all is. When we bend—or straight-up ignore—our boundaries and say yes when we want or need to say no, we end up so tired, hungry, tapped-out, and stressed-out that we lose our keys or our mind or our temper with our kids.

And then we blame ourselves for that too.

Just to be very clear, putting ourselves first isn't always possible, and that's OK. That's part of the deal when you're a parent, and it doesn't necessarily mean you're shitting on yourself. Life happens and we do our best with what we have. But when we consistently ignore our own needs because a) we believe our children's needs always take precedence over our own, b) we don't feel like we deserve any better, c) we think we have something to atone for, and/or d) we've completely blurred the line between

Super important point: First arrows aren't second arrows (and vice versa). Remembering the difference between first and second arrows is crucial to your self-compassion practice. Here's the short version: First arrows are the shit that happens to you and second arrows are how you think about—and respond to—that shit.

Crappy childhood? First arrow. Blaming yourself for struggling with parenting because you have zero role models? Second arrow.

Diagnosis of clinical depression? First arrow. Feeling like a shitty parent because you don't have the energy or desire to parent the way you want to? Second arrow all the way.

self-care and self-improvement and we truly believe that if we could just be better and do better, life would be less chaotic, well, that's just a bunch of second-arrow BS right there.

The Third Arrow of Denial and Distraction

And then, of course, there's a third arrow.

Because of course there freaking is.

We pull out our quiver of third arrows, the arrows of denial and distraction, when the pain of the first and second arrows gets too overwhelming. We do whatever it takes, often reactively and instinctively and generally without even realizing it, to just not think about whatever's going on. And there's absolutely nothing wrong with checking out from reality from time to time; in fact, it can be a highly effective coping mechanism. We all need a little time to sip our coffee, stare at the wall, or binge a few episodes of our favorite show.

Until, that is, our nightly glass of wine becomes three, or we're eating an entire tray of our feelings instead of just one cookie. Our compulsive eating, shopping, gambling, endless scrolling, porn watching, exercising, and busyness not only don't solve the problem, but they also reinforce the belief that we can't handle our darkest impulses or emotions. (Which, for the record, we totally can.) While those third arrows may offer a temporary respite from the first and second arrows, they make for a pretty shitty Band-Aid. Over time, third-arrow behaviors can put our jobs, relationships, health, and daily functioning at risk. Even as they're distracting us from the chaos, pain, and shame of our lives, they're opening us up to a whole new round of first and second arrows. And the cycle just keeps going.

The sharper our second arrows are, the more likely we'll be to bust out the third one because screw that stupid hike and stupid mini-golfing and that stupid ranger and our stupid kids who can't hold their stupid poop and that stupid-ass happy hiker family and their stupid-ass songs and screw it all. We can't control the chaos and we're just so tired of trying so hard and having it all fall apart anyway and we just don't want to think about any of it, so we space out on the couch, turn on a show while we thumb through our phone, throw back a beer or four, stay up way too late, and pretend like none of it ever happened. Fortunately, the fewer second arrows we sling at ourselves, the less likely we'll be to resort to third-arrow behaviors, which makes life and parenting so much easier.

Thwack thwack thwack.

This book is going to focus on noticing and changing our second-arrow habits, which will not only lessen the pain of the first arrow, but also make it less likely that we'll fall into third arrow behaviors. However, if you're struggling with any kind of addiction—if you're pinned down by a third arrow—please know that a) you're not alone and b) help is possible. Getting help isn't always easy, especially for busy parents who may often have limited time, energy, and money, but it's worth it. Thanks to online counseling options, therapy is more available than ever; see Chapter 5 for more information on how to connect with a licensed mental health practitioner.

How All These Arrows of Self-Contempt Make Parenting Harder and Less Fun

It's so tempting to believe that we can harass ourselves into being better parents. I mean, wouldn't it be great if that thing we're already doing so naturally actually worked? It would be super handy if that second arrow somehow magically healed our injuries and injected caffeine, patience, and the solution to that sixth-grade algebra problem directly into our bloodstream. Sadly, it just doesn't work that way. Regardless of what your evil aunt, jerk of a high school soccer coach, or sadistic boss might have you believe, bullying never leads to better behavior. Sure, we can terrify ourselves into temporary submission, but the results never last, and we end up back at Square 1, but it's more like Square −1, because now we're left with a bunch of open wounds.

Not only does treating ourselves like crap rarely lead to our desired outcome, but spending all day, every day, believing that we're failing at the most important work of our lives impacts our mental, emotional, and physical well-being in a variety of shitty ways.

We feel more confused and less confident about our parenting decisions and abilities when we're constantly doubting ourselves. After all, why would you trust the judgment of some idiot who keeps screwing up? And then we feel all stuck and confused and our parenting gets all tight and rigid. We can't stay calm or think clearly or creatively, and we end up resorting to arbitrary rules, inflexible reactions, and unwinnable power struggles. Basically, our self-contempt makes it far more likely that we'll default to our most unhelpful parenting reactions.

All of this causes tension in our family, and the more stressed and overwhelmed we are, the more likely we are to react impulsively and irritably and generally behave in the very ways we feel so ashamed of. This makes it hard to sleep at night, which makes us more prone to depression and anxiety. Or maybe we've been dealing with mental health issues since forever, and now they're just worse. Either way, it's hard not to feel depressed and anxious when we know we're going to berate, belittle, and shame ourselves for every choice we make and every unexpected, unpleasant, or downright awful outcome.

And it's not just our thoughts and feelings that are impacted; our self-contempt isn't good for our bodies either. Self-defeating thoughts and self-deprecating behaviors can lead to a whole variety of health problems, including crappy sleep, higher blood pressure, headaches, muscle tension, gastrointestinal problems, weight gain, trouble with memory and focus, and all that weird shit that happens to your body when it's all stressed-out.

It sucks.

The ability to remind yourself that you're not a monster or a freak or a failure, that we're all in this together, is one of the most powerful ways to treat yourself with kindness and ease the shame. You're just a human being trying to raise another human being in a crazy, complicated, and super chaotic world, and none of us really know what we're doing. Some of us are just better at faking it.

Nature, Nurture, and Now: Why We Think We Suck

Given that shooting ourselves with second and third arrows only makes things worse, one has to wonder how and when we humans started berating ourselves for the totally normal (albeit epically sucky) chaos of life. And why the heck do we keep at it?

The short answer is this: Who the hell knows?

I'm not just being flip here; the truth is that there is often no clear explanation for much of our behavior, including why we're so damn harsh on ourselves. And that's OK, because we don't necessarily need to understand the *why* in order to change the *what.*

Having said that, much of our shitty self-talk and self-deprecating behavior can be attributed to some combination of nature, nurture, and our lives now. As you read through the following list of factors that contribute to our self-contempt, please note that "You're a horrible person and you really do suck more than everyone else" is nowhere to be found. I will hammer this point home until the end of days (or at least until the end of this book), but whether you think your shitty parent stories are true, they're not kind and they're not useful. Seeing as how kind and useful are totally the jam of this book, let's focus on them, shall we?

Nature: We're Wired for Connection, Comparison, and Catastrophizing

As crazy as it sounds, there's an evolutionary advantage to all those shitty second arrows. Human beings are wired to stay connected to their communities, and so much of our seemingly senseless behavior (including treating ourselves like crap) stems from that primal need. The reality is that our ancestors who were either a) self-righteous dicks or b) super weird or different were likely to find themselves wandering the savannah alone and at the mercy of the first hungry saber-toothed tiger to cross their path.

So it came to pass that those cave parents who were consistently self-deprecating and doing their best to fit in were far less likely to get kicked to the prehistoric curb and far more likely to stay alive long enough to raise self-deprecating babies. And now, whether we realize it or not, every time we talk shit about ourselves, we're securing our place in the tribe.

Putting ourselves down in front of our fellow parents is just one way to stay connected to our community. Making sure we fit in is another one, and that requires us to keep an eye on what everyone else is up to—how they're feeding their children, putting them to bed at night, teaching them to tie their shoes, and making sure they pass social studies. While we may get some helpful information and insights from our fellow parents, comparisons are inevitable, and comparisons usually suck—at least for the comparer. Although approaching every interaction with a mental yardstick rarely feels good, we keep doing it because it's the easiest way to determine, maintain, and possibly even improve our social status.

There's no question that all the shitty self-talk and constant comparisons are totally not awesome. Even if we don't buy into everything we're saying about ourselves—even if we don't actually think we're shitty parents—the more frequently we repeat something, the more likely we are to believe it.

However, staying connected to our community is crucial, but only when said community consists of actual people who share their experiences honestly and authentically, and from whom you can reap the benefits of being part of a tribe, whether it's a ride to the recital or a reality check. It's not so helpful when your "community"—those folks you can't help but compare yourself to—includes parenting experts and social media mavens who may live in completely different worlds, have access to completely different resources, and share only highly filtered and carefully curated versions of their lives, which generally have nothing to do with yours.

Their advice might be helpful and relevant, or it may just be another crap map. Either way, we shouldn't be comparing ourselves to them anymore than we should compare ourselves to pandas or potatoes. But man is it hard to remember that when we're staring at a video of a smiling parent, happily feeding their cooperative children brussels sprouts as they share their story of overcoming clutter in just one afternoon and finishing their first marathon in under five hours.

Look, self-contempt and comparison wouldn't be so bad if we could find a way to let it all go, to notice those thoughts without actually taking their bait (which I'll teach you to do over the course of this book). But that leaves us with our tendency toward catastrophizing, or assuming the worst will happen. It's not that we're gluttons for punishment; rather, our brains are wired to look for, notice, and remember the threats and failures in life, both real and perceived. As much as this sucks, it actually kind of makes sense; those cave folk whose brains led them to assume that squiggly thing on the ground was a snake instead of a stick and jumped out of the way were far more likely to survive than those who leaned down to pick it up. And of those anxiety-prone cave folk, the ones who obsessively remembered and replayed the stick/snake situation over and over again were far more likely to react quickly and decisively the next time they saw something similar on the ground. In addition, their children were far more likely to survive, which, evolutionarily speaking, is the whole point of our existence.

Basically, the cave moms and dads who were extra hypervigilant and reactive, doing whatever it took to keep their kids alive, were the ones whose DNA stuck around long enough to pass on their anxious, obsessive, keep-their-kids-alive-at-all-costs parenting style to their children, and their children's children, and every generation, right up to today, to you and me and every other parent with a twitchy eye, blossoming anxiety disorder, and tendency to focus on the worst, including in ourselves.

Another powerful factor at play is confirmation bias. The deeply human tendency to hold ourselves responsible for that which is beyond our control is both a cause and effect of the shitty parent stories we tell ourselves. Once we've decided, for whatever reason, that we suck, our brains continue to seek out, interpret, and remember evidence in ways that confirm that belief. This doesn't mean it's true, and it doesn't mean there's anything wrong with us. It's just how our brains work.

Nurture: We Grew Up in an Imperfect World

Even those of us who had relatively "normal" childhoods were still criticized, bullied, or harassed at some point in our lives. Maybe you were too skinny or too chubby, or you had a name that was hard to pronounce, or you were the only LGBTQ kid or child of color in your class. And even though Adult You can look back at Kid You and see that that your experiences weren't your fault, they were just the predictable (if shitty) outcome of living in a deeply imperfect and intolerant world, Kid You didn't know that at the time. Kid You only knew that you were the one who didn't fit in, so clearly it was your fault. And now some part of Adult You still thinks it's (whatever it is) your fault, even though it's totally not and never was.

On the off chance you weren't different at all (or, more likely, just lucky enough to have a hidable difference), that didn't mean you were off the hook. Whether it came from a parent, a sibling, or that punk in seventh grade who kept snapping your bra or shoving you in a locker, someone treated you like crap and made you feel incapable, incompetent, or worthless. That's not to say that your parent, sibling, or seventh-grade bully hated you or was inherently evil; like you, they were also raised in a culture, family, or community that taught or modeled that harassment and contempt are acceptable responses to life's challenges and chaos. Whatever the reason, whatever they said or did likely had nothing to do with you and maybe didn't make any damn sense at all, but taking other people's opinions far more seriously than we should is a side effect of the human condition and an especially strong one when it comes to kids.

And that's just the story for those folks who didn't have traumatic childhoods. For those of us who weren't so fortunate, a history of trauma, neglect, and abuse can lead to entrenched feelings of inadequacy and shame. Children tend to blame themselves for the worst that happens to them, even though it's never their fault. As painful as it may be for kids to think that they're the reason for their parent's rage or rejection, it's safer than believing that their parent, the one person on the planet who is supposed to love and protect them, might hurt them or can't take care of them. And those old stories can be damn hard to shake, no matter how many years go by.

The bottom line is that we all have a childhood story, and most of us have lots of them. Whether it was one especially brutal experience that rewired your thinking or the constant repetition that wore you down and left you filled with self-doubt and shame, any underlying beliefs you may have developed about your own competence and worthiness may still be sticking around, making those second and third arrows sharper than ever. Even when we know that it's bullshit and fundamentally the other person's problem, on some level, it's still damn hard to tune out those voices.

Our Lives Now: Parenting Is Chaos

We're all painfully aware that raising kids is full of first arrows. These can range from the basic challenges (how and when to feed them, put them to sleep, treat minor illnesses and infections, etc.); the what-we-thought-were-basics-but-apparently-aren't (how to talk to our kids, get them to help around the house, and schedule their after-school activities, for example), and the purely mind-blowing (when to give them a smartphone, how to prevent eating disorders, and what, exactly, are we supposed to do about school shootings? That's not a rhetorical question. I would really like to know.) And it's not just that we're supposed to worry about things we hadn't even previously realized were things at all, but that the advice keeps changing. If we're still doing what we did yesterday, we're probably doing it wrong.

Good parents, we've been led to believe, don't live chaotic lives. They have their shit together and their heads screwed on straight and a truly fantastic color-coded calendaring system. But don't be fooled. Just getting through the day is often a challenge for even the most organized, energized, rested, and clear-thinking among us. And most of us parents aren't functioning at our best. We're exhausted from trying to be so damn perfect, parenting through a freaking pandemic, balancing our work and home lives, and not having the information, support, and resources we need. And, for all the reasons we just discussed, one of the most popular, if super unhelpful, conclusions that our brains jump to when we're tired and stressed is that if we're not perfect, we suck.

How the Second and Third Arrows Impact Our Kids

No matter how hard we might work to hide our second- and third-arrow habits from our kids, we can't. Our children absolutely know when we're freaking out, stressing out, or shutting down. And here's the thing about kids: They're incredibly self-centered. They default to assuming that they have a central role in whatever's going on, and they struggle to keep other people's perspectives and needs in mind. That doesn't mean there's anything wrong with your kids or they're budding psychopaths. It's a developmental stage, and they'll grow out of it. What it does mean is that as they watch us (and not to sound incredibly creepy or anything, but they're always freaking watching us) and try to make sense of our tense, rigid, second-arrow reactions, they're prone to blaming themselves or assuming they're at fault for whatever's going on.

Thwack. Thwack.

Our kids can nail themselves with second arrows before they even know what the first arrow is.

But it's not just all in our kids' heads. Our behavior impacts them directly. As the noted author Wayne Dyer once said, "When you squeeze an orange, you get orange juice." When we get squeezed, whatever's on the inside is what's going to come out. And if we're filled with shame and blame and then our kids squeeze us—by crying through the night or biting their little sister or refusing to get into the damn car or flipping their plate and storming off in the middle of dinner or who the hell knows—we ooze our contempt all over them. The levels of tension and conflict in our families shoot up, which weakens our relationship with our kids and makes it even harder to deal effectively with the actual issue. And none of this is because we're shitty parents. It's because we can't give our children what we don't have, and most of us don't have anything better. At least not yet.

And that's just the second arrow. When our kids see us react to difficult moments by stressing out, checking out, or shutting down, they may develop the same habits over time. Each time we space out in front of a screen or eat or drink too much, for example, in response to life's snafus, not only are they learning how to do the same thing, but they're not learning any other more effective and empathic coping skills either.

So even if you're still suspicious of all this self-compassion stuff or you're not yet ready to forgive yourself, hang in there. Fake it till ya make it. Your whole family will benefit.

CHAPTER TWO

Life's a Beach and Then We Freak Out

Thanks to our wiring, our upbringing, and the insanity of modern parenthood, many of us are suffering from Shitty Parent Syndrome. That means we take responsibility for situations beyond our control, blame ourselves for the snafus, and hold ourselves to impossible standards regardless of what kind of shitstorm we're facing. And once we get in the habit of pulling out the crap map or shooting ourselves with second arrows, even everyday decisions and dilemmas (such as what to put in your daughter's lunchbox, how to get your son to remember to bring his cleats to soccer practice, or whether or not to let your teen go to that party they've been nagging you about) can feel like a referendum on what kind of parent we are. Of course, the minute the situations get even slightly more complex, as they always do, we get completely lost. The chaos starts to feel like a crisis, and we freak out.

I think of these as Beach Day Moments. They happen all the time, and they seem like they should be relatively straightforward and easy to handle. Most of us don't even realize how stressful and insidious they can be. But when we can recognize the Beach Day chaos for what it is, we'll be far less likely to blame ourselves for what happens and how we react.

Let's say it's the day of the annual sandcastle-building contest on the coast, an outing that you and your family have been looking forward to ever since you had an amazing time last year. But the weather is calling for an unusually hot and muggy day, with poor air quality because of raging wildfires on the other side of the country. Normally you might not be too concerned, but your daughter's asthma has been acting up, and you're worried about her breathing in the hot, smoggy air. You're trying to figure out what to do.

It should be a simple decision—to go to the beach or not. But as you and your family try to figure out what to do, it starts falling apart faster than you can put anything together. Maybe your mother calls or texts; she's concerned about the smoke and her granddaughter's health. Perhaps she even reminds you about the last time you took your daughter out on a hot day, sending your guilt and shame through the roof. And so you respond as any reasonable grown child would; you lose your shit and hang up on her.

Or maybe instead of a call from your mother, that dinging on your phone is a message from a colleague. They're super apologetic about bothering you on a weekend morning, but they have a quick question about a slide they're working on for your big presentation next week. Even though you know this is an issue that can wait until Monday, you decide to call them quickly while your partner figures out what to do, which, of course, pisses off your partner.

The possibilities for how this day could go are endless; maybe you try to put off the decision as long as possible in hopes that the weather forecast will change, but you can't do that forever because if you wait too long the parking lot at the beach will fill up. Or maybe your daughter won't stop nagging you about going, and it's stressing you out so you explode at your spouse for leaving their dishes in the sink. Perhaps you promise your daughter you'll finally buy her that video game she's been wanting in hopes of distracting her from the meltdown you just can't handle today, even though you swore you weren't going to bribe her like that anymore. Or maybe you pull out your phone, desperately searching for a detailed, localized weather forecast for the shore or data about the impact of smoky air on asthma, which, of course, yields little useful information or perhaps too much contradictory information. Either way, you're left feeling as confused and powerless as ever.

Damnit. Your Shitty Parent Syndrome has flared up.

You're lost, so you reach for a map, perhaps the only map at your disposal. Your crap map. You begin to tell yourself that you're not managing the situation well. A good parent would be able to either get their family to the beach or somehow create something equally magical at home, like that woman on Instagram who filled her sunporch with real sand, inflatable palm trees, and a kiddie pool. Except you don't have a freaking sunporch, and the thought of bringing sand into your house makes you break out in hives.

You can't help but believe that you should be able to resolve all of this calmly and easily, without snapping at your partner, hanging up on your mother, or bribing your kid. A good parent would fix the problem, not freak out about it. But you're not doing any of that, and you end up feeling like shit. And so another chapter is added to our ever-expanding story about all the ways in which you're failing your kids, your family, and yourself.

But what if there was a different way to understand these Beach Day Moments? What if instead of seeing them as relatively simple situations that we should be able to instinctively or easily resolve in a way that keeps everyone happy, we were able to step back and see the variety of complex dynamics at play? What if we could get some clarity on the chaos rather than blaming ourselves for it? In order to do this, we need to dig a little deeper into what really happened.

Maybe the cat vomited in your bedroom in the middle of the night, and it took you two hours to get back to sleep, so you're exhausted and a bit overwhelmed by the prospect of packing for a big outing. You've heard about possible layoffs at work and as much as you try not to think about your job over the weekend, you can't stop stressing about it. If you were to stay home, you might be able to sneak in a little work while your daughter is distracted. But she's been struggling in school and you think a Beach Day could go a long way toward cheering her up. Besides, this wouldn't be the first time her asthma has kept her from a fun activity, and you want her to grow up believing that she can do anything she sets her mind to.

Despite your fatigue and stress, you really want to make this Beach Day happen. You're determined to step up your parenting and spend some quality time with your spouse. You haven't been making many of those family memories lately, and you've been feeling guilty as hell about it. And as much as you love your kiddo, you just don't have the energy to deal with another epic explosion followed by a day of sulking and whining, which is inevitably what will happen if you cancel the trip.

And so, as worried as you are about your daughter's health, you try to talk yourself into it. You could make the outing a little shorter than you had previously planned; just enough to keep her happy without really screwing up her lungs. Maybe your daughter's asthma won't get triggered; you did just start her on a new inhaler a few weeks ago. But then you're just not sure. Is it worth the risk? Once her asthma gets going, your little girl can end up coughing for weeks and when things get really bad, she has to take steroids, the side effects of which are epically sucky. Not only do you worry about your daughter's long-term health each time her asthma flares up, but she'll inevitably have to miss school and you and your partner will end up negotiating over who gets to go to work and who has to stay home.

The chaos is becoming a crisis.

As stressful as it sounds, this fake beach day is actually a relatively straightforward scenario, one that assumes you have only one child's needs to consider, a parenting partner to help you, a job that provides income and health insurance, and access to life-saving health care. Many parents deal with far more complicated balancing acts on a regular basis.

There are as many versions of this story as there are families. Maybe yours isn't about a beach day and asthma. Maybe it's about a trip to a museum or a family holiday, or just even trying to get your kid to school in the morning. And maybe your child doesn't have asthma, but they struggle with other developmental or health issues such as anxiety, angry outbursts, or challenges related to neurodivergence. Regardless of the details, these situations have one thing in common: They leave us feeling powerless, defensive, anxious, and confused as we blame ourselves for the chaos.

These beach day decisions call on us to weigh competing values, benefits, and risks and make the best possible choice from a range of crappy ones while holding ourselves to ridiculously high standards. And they happen nearly constantly, in both small and significant ways. Sometimes our families really are in crisis, and sometimes it's just super unpleasant "everyday" chaos that's taken on far more meaning than it warrants. Questions about when to sleep train or potty train aren't just about how to get through the next developmental milestone; they carry the weight of your child's mental and emotional growth and health. The choice of whether to take a forgotten lunch or band instrument isn't just about the logistics of the day, but about whether we're helping or hindering our children's development and sense of self-sufficiency. And even if we have the financial flexibility to decide if we want to stay home with the kids or go back to work, it's never about the money or our own sanity; the wrong choice could screw up our kids forever. And screen time? That's the ultimate Pandora's box. (And in case you're not familiar with that particular Greek myth, allow me to remind you that by opening said box, Pandora unleashed a torrent of physical and emotional curses upon humanity, so yeah, that screen time metaphor actually makes a terrifying amount of sense.)

What started out as a question about how to spend a few weekend hours has quickly become entangled with concerns about your daughter's mental health and success at school, your relationship with her and with your partner, your sense of yourself as a competent and connected parent, and your child's very ability to breathe. And you haven't even finished your first cup of coffee.

Exhaustion. Work stress. Family stress. Your daughter's health and well-being. Your sense of yourself as a caring, capable parent. So many triggers. So many stressors. So many freaking first arrows. Only one way to get this right—a successful, healthy day at the beach—and so many ways to get it wrong. At some point it just becomes too much. Your nervous system gets overloaded. You are no longer struggling with a parenting decision. You're facing a threat to yourself and your child as well.

All those Beach Day arrows have triggered your fight or flight response.

How We Freak Out: Fight, Flight, Freeze, Flip Out, Fix, and Fawn

As the world has gotten more complex, so has our repertoire of reactions. Our survival instincts are no longer limited to fight or flight; they've expanded to include freeze, flip out, fix, and fawn. These responses show up in a variety of ways in our lives, and there's nothing inherently wrong with any of them. Sometimes they're helpful, such as when your child won't stop wheezing and you need to rush her to the hospital or when you grab your toddler just as they're about to dash into traffic. But when our freak-outs are triggered by our second-arrow thinking, by our belief that we could and should be in control of an inherently chaotic situation, parenting gets harder, more stressful, and less manageable than it might have been otherwise.

In those moments, our reactions often feel out of control and disproportionate to the situation. We assume we should be able to get and stay calm and patient regardless of what's happening, and we feel like crap when we can't. But when we can see chaos for what it is—just another freaking situation normal, all fucked up—we'll be far less likely to freak out about it. And learning to recognize our reactive patterns—our fight, flight, freeze, flip out, fix, and fawn reactions—and remembering that these are instinctual and not indicative of our parenting abilities, will help ease some of the shame.

As you read through the list and descriptions that follow, try to notice which tendencies seem familiar to you. Are you more of a fighter or a fawner? Do you tend to take off (physically, mentally, or emotionally) in difficult times? Keep in mind that you may resort to different reactions—even over the course of a single day—depending on what the trigger is, who or what triggered you, and how energetic or exhausted you are. And please try to remember: This isn't about right or wrong; it's just about getting to know your own habit patterns so you're less likely to be surprised and sidelined by them.

Fight. This isn't about actually punching a bear or an obnoxious soccer parent in the face (except, of course, when it is). In most cases, our fights take the form of instigating or intensifying conflict with the people in our lives, including friends, family, the schmuck who stole the parking spot you had clearly been waiting for, and some bozo online who absolutely needs to be reminded to stay in his lane. Now, I'm not saying every conflict is an instinctive or unhelpful reaction; there are certainly times when disputes or disagreements are warranted. I'm just saying that the next time you go all claws out, fangs bared at some asshat on Twitter or at your kiddo for leaving their dirty socks in the middle of the kitchen floor, it might be a red flag warning that you're in the middle of a freak-out.

Flight. It's not often that we physically run away from our children (although it can be tempting at times). More often, this looks like staying late at work, opening a bottle of wine as soon as the kids are in bed, locking ourselves in the bathroom with a bag of chips, or disappearing into our phones. We can run away from the painful experiences and emotions of our lives in so many different ways, including losing ourselves in exercise, shopping, drinking, using drugs, or online gaming and gambling. We lose ourselves in perfectionism, in our job, our hobbies, or volunteer activities, or our extended family obligations—anything that keeps us from having to face the chaos or feel the confusion, overwhelm, fear, shame, and blame that show up far too frequently. Again, not necessarily a bad thing—until it is.

Freeze. Most of us think of freezing as the wide-eyed, unable to move, deer-in-the-headlights moment when the gears grind to a screeching halt and we literally can't get out of the way. While this can happen when there's an actual physical threat to ourselves or our children, the freeze reaction can also show up as procrastination, boredom, zoning out, feeling emotionally or psychologically numb or stuck, unsure what to do next, or feeling unable to make even the most basic decisions. Finally, in some situations (especially for trauma survivors) freezing can also manifest as disassociating or disconnecting from reality.

Flip out. Emotional instability, outbursts, snapping, losing your shit—whatever you call it, this is exactly what it sounds like. We all have our own version of flipping out, including shouting, screaming, and swearing, either in person, online, or over texts or emails. (YES, IT IS POSSIBLE TO SHOUT TYPE.) Other folks burst into tears, slam doors, or throw remote controls. Our feelings just get too big, too overwhelming, and we explode. The explosions are often followed by self-doubt, self-judgment, irritability, and snappiness.

Fix. Fixing is one of my go-to moves, and it's taken me a long time to realize it can be quite unhelpful. Fixing reactions can include seeking advice, consulting experts, obsessively reading parenting books (or, in my case, writing them), researching online articles, giving advice, planning, making lists, shopping for just the right thing, micro-managing your child's life, or trying to take responsibility for that which is beyond your control. Fixing is a tricky one, because many of these behaviors can be super helpful, depending on your motivation, state of mind, or context. We'll talk more about this in the coming chapters, but it's important to get clear on whether you're trying to fix something that's actually broken and fixable (like a fractured ankle) or you're trying to fix something that is neither broken nor fixable (such as the challenge of accepting your child as a person whose life choices don't align with the dreams you have for them), as so many of the challenges in life are.

Fawn. This one may surprise you but bear with me. Fawning shows up as people pleasing, currying favor, and bending over backward to give friends, family, colleagues, and community members whatever they want or need to keep them happy. It makes sense when you think about it; if you can't fight off the bear, you might as well do whatever you can to keep it content, right? And when the bear is actually your crazy toddler or cranky teenager, it's not hard to see why so many parents end up giving in to their children's demands or requests in a desperate attempt to make them happy, or at the very least, end the tantrum. Regardless of the details, fawning generally involves weakening or disrespecting our own boundaries, which can be just another form of self-condemnation.

Let's get back to the Beach Day. Now that you're aware of all the first arrows flying at you and how your nervous system might be interpreting them as threats, the situation looks pretty different. Your reactions aren't evidence of your failings; they're just what happens when your little meat computer of a brain freaks out, perhaps by hanging up on your mom (fight), bailing on the situation to help a colleague (flight), procrastinating on making a decision (freeze), snapping at your spouse (flip out), obsessively checking the forecast (fix), or bribing your child (fawn). What each of these have in common is that they're driven by an underlying sense, conscious or otherwise, that shit is falling apart (whether or not it actually is) and that it's all our responsibility

Bodhipaksa, the noted meditation teacher, refers to our brains as meat computers. Yes, the metaphor is a little gross, but it's also a useful reminder that as incredible as our minds can be, at the end of the day, they're just water, fat, protein, and carbs. They're just little brain burgers doing the best they can with what they have, which may not always be enough.

to fix it (which we often can't), and our fault if we can't (which it rarely is).

Maybe you'll figure out a way to get to the beach, maybe you won't. Maybe you'll look back on the situation and decide you made the right call, or maybe you won't. Who knows? Maybe your daughter will have an epic meltdown or maybe she'll manage to keep it together. Regardless of how it all shakes out, parenting becomes much easier and less stressful when you can step back from the chaos and judgment and remember that you don't have to solve every problem and that you don't have to be a perfect parent in order to be a good one. The ability to put away your crap map and dodge the second arrow will give you the head- and heart-space to show up for the challenges of parenting feeling calm, clear, creative, and confident.

CHAPTER THREE

Self-Compassion Is Your Secret Sauce

Parenting is, by definition, chaotic. It's loud and messy and inconsistent and stressful as shit. And maybe it wouldn't be such a problem, except for one thing: We naturally assume that chaos is what happens when things go wrong.

Except it's not. Because if you look up *chaos* in the dictionary, you'll see it isn't just about disorder and confusion. It also refers to the inherent unpredictability in the behavior of a natural system. Our families are those natural systems, and the chaos is *inherent,* as in a permanent quality or feature.

Chaos isn't things going wrong; it's just life doing its thing.

This description of raising children makes so much sense; the more people you add to a family, the more chaos you're going to introduce, especially when some of those people tend to pee in the potted plants and fling their fish sticks across the kitchen. The point here is that chaos is normal. Unpredictability, confusion, disorder, and disorganization are part of the parenting deal. They always have been, and they always will be. Self-compassion is the key to accepting the chaos of parenting with wisdom and humor rather than berating ourselves for our imperfections.

Compassion as an intentional practice can seem super weird at first, to be sure. The first time I was introduced to self-compassion, I nearly burst out laughing when the instructor in the mindfulness class I was taking suggested sending ourselves happy wishes. I mean, who comes up with this crap? I couldn't help but picture a stream of puffy cartoon hearts and sparkly rainbows flying right at me. I didn't need happy wishes; I needed to learn how to get my shit together instead of losing it. But I had signed up for a mindfulness-based stress reduction (MBSR) course in hopes of learning how to be calmer and more patient, and I didn't think my fellow participants—all of whom appeared to be 100 percent on board with this lovey-dovey baloney—would appreciate such a blatant display of disrespect, so I somehow managed to keep my mouth shut. Even so, the petulant child in me (who's actually just a petulant adult) could barely keep my eyeballs from rolling right out of my head and steadfastly refused to put my hand over my heart. There was no way I was doing any of it.

I know I'm not the only one to have such misconceptions about what self-compassion is and how and why it's worth our precious time and energy. Most folks assume it's some combination of syrupy-sweet affirmations, self-centered navel-gazing, and myopic self-love. Sure, it may offer some temporary and thin veneer of ease or happiness in the moment, but if we really want to make lasting change in our lives, we need to step up, buckle down, stop screwing around, and get our shit together.

Or so we tell ourselves.

Except here's the question I had to ask myself and that you might also want to consider: How's that working for you? Seriously. Have you actually been able to bully yourself into better behavior? Second arrow yourself into submission? Harass yourself into becoming the kind of parent you think you should be? None of that worked for me—and not for lack of effort, I assure you. If you're anything like every human I've ever met, it's not going to work for you either. Letting go of any biases and erroneous beliefs you might hold about self-compassion is a crucial step toward putting away the crap map, avoiding the second arrows, and turning toward connection, curiosity, and kindness.

What Self-Compassion Is Not

There's a crazy long list of what self-compassion isn't. It's not about bolstering ourselves with forced affirmations, pretending like we never screwed up when we clearly did, or telling ourselves to just suck it up, buttercup. It's critically important that we learn to recognize the range of imposter emotions and experiences, because while they can help you feel better in the moment, they're quite different—and not nearly as effective—as self-compassion.

It's Not Just a Hippie-Dippie Fantasy. Self-compassion isn't just a nice idea that some happy person with their head in the clouds came up with while sipping kombucha and tuning their wind chimes. It's an active choice to respond to our most painful moments with connection, curiosity, and kindness, and there's a significant and growing body of high-quality research to support it. If you're interested in understanding more about the science of self-compassion, check out the resources in Chapter 9.

It's Not Self-Pity. Let's go back to that ill-fated hike and what a pity party might look like: you, plopping down on a log and starting to blubber because you just can't handle the whole situation. "I'm the worst," you cry to your family, "I can't do anything right. Why do I even try? You all were right. I should have never planned this horrible hike in the first place. I'm a terrible partner and an even worse parent. Go on. Take the kids mini-golfing. Just leave me here. I deserve to be lost in these godforsaken woods."

It's easy to see how self-pity can get confused with self-compassion. Both involve acknowledging our own suffering, to be sure. But unlike self-compassion, which is about trying to ease our own pain, self-pity is about wallowing in it. It's when we get all wound up and worked up about how miserable and pathetic we are and how terrible our lives are and how we deserve every single shitty arrow the universe keeps sending our way. We become completely absorbed in our own struggles and suffering, unable to consider any other perspectives or possibilities. While it can feel good in the moment to melt into our misery, eventually the pity party will end, as every party does. And all we've done is annoy everyone around us and reinforce our underlying beliefs that we do, in fact, suck.

It's Not Self-Indulgence. This is a variation of the pity-party in which we decide that we're the worst and we'll never be anything but the worst so screw it, why not just have another beer or pint of ice cream or finally buy that overpriced wolf-howling-at-the-moon shirt we've been eyeing? We zoom right past the self-contempt so quickly we don't even notice it. Instead, we head straight to the kitchen or the keyboard or wherever we think we'll find something—anything—to keep us from thinking and feeling all the shitty, unpleasant thoughts and feelings we know are lurking around that one particular corner of our existence we're doing our damnedest not to visit.

Just like self-pity, the third arrow of giving in to our every want and whim can be a super effective distraction, at least in the moment. But the relief is temporary, and the faster, further, and more frequently we run from our darkest corners, the more we're reinforcing—whether we realize it or not—the false belief that whatever we may find there is so offensive and deeply problematic that there's no way we'll be able to handle it.

Self-compassion, on the other hand, calls on us to face whatever is in the dark corners, but instead of judging it, we meet it with understanding, acceptance, and forgiveness.

It's Not Letting Yourself Off the Hook. Most of us are stuck in the habit of hurling second arrows right after the first ones. If we've made a mistake or a bad judgment call, we think the most effective response is to come down hard on ourselves—perhaps with harsh criticism, angry outbursts, and ongoing reminders of just how screwed up we'll forever be if we don't make some serious changes and fast.

Not only is this total bullshit, but it also promotes the pervasive and super problematic belief that treating ourselves with any kind of compassion is just letting ourselves off the hook. Shouldn't we pay for our mistakes? If there is no discipline, no punishment, and no recourse, then how will we ever learn our lesson? And what will stop us from screwing everything up all over again?

The reality is that self-compassion has nothing to with burying our heads in the sand or sweeping everything under the rug.

In fact, it's just the opposite. When we trust that we'll respond to ourselves with understanding and acceptance—regardless of how hard and fast the shit may be hitting the fan—we can be honest and realistic about whatever's going on. From that place of insight and calm clarity, we can figure out what's actually going on and move forward in the most intentional way possible.

This question of whether to discipline our children or not comes up frequently as parents struggle to help their children to slow down, make better choices, behave appropriately, and cooperate with our requests. Should we lay the smack down, take away their screens, and put their tiny hineys in time-out so they can think about what they've done? Or respond with compassion and understanding? The answer is actually both. We can connect to our children, get curious about their experiences, and treat them with kindness—even as we set limits, hold expectations, and discipline them appropriately, if necessary. More on this in Chapter 8.

It's Not Self-Esteem. Self-esteem is just a trendy term for the opinion we hold of ourselves; self-evaluation would probably be more accurate. When our self-esteem is high, we feel good, we believe in ourselves, and we know we're doing our best. There's nothing wrong with any of this, except, of course, for the one big thing that's wrong with it. At the end of the day, these evaluations of our own worthiness are almost entirely dependent on external circumstances and success, which we may have limited or no control over. We can make all the right choices and work our asses off and things can still fall apart. We can be minding our own damn business and bad news might still land in our laps and blow up our lives—and our self-esteem.

The extra tricky thing about parental self-esteem is that it can get completely tangled up with our kids' good behavior and success, or lack thereof. We feel good about ourselves when our kids take their first steps or bring home a strong report card or let their sibling sit in the front seat without a fight. We feel good when they feel good. And that would be all fine and dandy if we were raising perfect children who never missed developmental milestones or drew on their bedroom walls or threw chairs in the middle of math class. But perfect doesn't exist, and when our sense of ourselves is dependent on how our kids are feeling and doing, things can go south real quick, and not because there's anything wrong with them or us. It's because judging ourselves based on outcomes rarely ends well.

Fortunately, self-compassion doesn't care about outcomes or achievements or how the kids are doing. Self-compassion is just about responding to our suffering with kindness and acceptance, no matter how shitty things get.

It's Not Self-Improvement. When we truly believe that all of life's challenges and chaos are our own damn fault, it's easy to understand why so many of us seek solace in self-improvement. If we could only get in better shape or learn to meditate or find the right parenting class or therapist, maybe we could finally pull ourselves together and become a better parent.

Now, this can get awfully confusing because exercise and parenting classes and meditation and therapy can all be incredibly helpful. These practices and habits are an important part of my life, and I frequently recommend them to others. But when our actions are driven by an unshakable sense, a core belief that we're fundamentally flawed and in need of improvement, self-improvement quickly becomes a second or even third arrow and even the best CrossFit class or self-help book can't take the sting out of that.

But when we approach these same behaviors from a place of care and compassion, and a desire to take care of—rather than fix—ourselves, well, it's a completely different experience. We're not shooting ourselves all over again; we're tending to our wounds and doing our best to avoid future first arrows whenever possible, all the while knowing that it will never be entirely possible, and *that's OK*. It's the difference between a friend telling us we look like shit and need to pull our lives together and that same friend taking the time to listen and inviting us to take a hike or join them in a meditation class. As the famous psychologist Carl Rogers once said, "The curious paradox is that when I accept myself just as I am, then I can change."

What Self-Compassion Is

Imagine if instead of a punk-ass gremlin constantly judging you, you had a friend. A friend who knows your whole history—every pissy, rageful, regretful thought you've ever had about parenting, every escape fantasy that's gotten you through the day, every time you wished your kids would just shut the hell up and leave you alone, every lie or rude comment, every time you fell off the wagon and broke your diet or your vows, all of it. And get this: They still love you. They still want to come chill at your kitchen table while you snap at your kids and stress about work and burn dinner beyond all recognition.

What if you could go to that friend every time you needed a reality check or a pep talk or a reminder that you're not the only one who gets lost in the weeds sometimes? Imagine all the ways in which having that friend with you could alleviate your shame, ease your doubt, and generally make your life easier.

As I'm sure you've realized by now, that friend is actually you. You can let go of the constant comparisons and self-judgment, reach out for support, get curious about your own experience, and be as kind to yourself as you would be to a good friend who was having a hard time.

Self-compassion is about recognizing the chaos of parenting for what it is—the inherent unpredictability of life with kids—and not blaming ourselves for any of it. It's about noticing when we're down and choosing not to kick ourselves yet again. Compassion helps us shift out of fight or flight mode and into tend and befriend. Tend and befriend isn't just some handy rhyme; it's an alternate evolutionary response to threats. While the fighters and warriors did their fighty and warry stuff, the folks back in the cave focused on keeping the babies safe (tend) and supporting one another (befriend).

Although tend and befriend evolved out of a fundamental need to keep the babies and baby-makers alive, it also happens to be a surprisingly useful way to deal with the roughest moments of modern parenting, even when survival isn't on the line. When we know our babies are healthy and safe, we can relax. And when we know we're not alone in keeping them safe or even just getting through an unstructured afternoon, parenting feels—and is—so much easier.

It may be tempting to assume that fight or flight is for dads and tend and befriend is mom territory. And this may have been true in the past, when gender identities and roles were more rigidly defined and men were out hunting while women farmed and swept the cave and tended the babies. But make no mistake about it, fathers have always cared for their children and mothers have always been willing to fight for them. And now, as increasing numbers of mothers are working outside the home and more and more fathers are taking a more active role in raising their children, life is crazy and chaotic for all of us. We're all fighting and fleeing and we can all shift into tend and befriend at any time.

It's possible that at this moment you're thinking to yourself, Hang on there, lady. I tend and befriend all the freaking time. I tend the crap out of my kids. I feed them and bathe them and drive their tiny hineys all over town and wipe their tears and drag them to dentist appointments and nag them about their homework and their screen time and all the freaking things. And when it comes to befriending, I'm doing the best I can. I call my mom twice a week and I chat up the other parents at pick-up and I go to poker night and I do all the things, so if tend and befriend is so damn useful, then why do I still feel like crap?

You (by which I mean, *I*) raise excellent points. You're working so hard and doing so much—for your kids and family and community and everyone else. And there's nothing wrong with that, except when you forget to tend to *yourself.* So now it's time to refocus some of that tend and befriend energy inward, and not by working harder or doing more—that is literally the exact opposite of what we're going for here—but by recognizing when you're stressed and struggling and choosing to take care of yourself. And each time you do that, you'll experience a ton of benefits.

Benefits of Self-Compassion

If someone tried to sell me self-compassion in a pill, I would read the list of benefits and assume it was a load of malarkey. Decreased anxiety and depression. Increased happiness and resilience. Stronger relationships and connections. Healthier behaviors and habits. More presence and patience with your children. Your car will be instantly paid off. OK, maybe not that last one, but the rest of them are real and backed by a strong and growing body of research.

It's like instead of pulling out a crap map, you've just pulled out one that feels pretty damn magical. Except it's not magic. It's just what happens when you've always got someone by your side, someone who's gotten completely lost with you before and they're always up for another hike, someone who's seen you flat out on the floor and still wants to stay for coffee. Given that relatively few of us have ever had someone like this in our lives, it might be pretty hard to imagine what it would feel like and how it would impact our sense of ourselves and how we move through the world. I get that. That's why self-compassion is a practice, a way of treating ourselves that we need to come back to over and over again, until eventually you don't have to imagine anything because you'll be living it.

The easiest way to understand the benefits of self-compassion is to go back to the chaos and confusion of Beach Day Moments. The stress, anxiety, tough choices, and competing needs trigger our freak-outs, which flood our bodies with stress hormones such as cortisol and adrenaline. Our muscles tighten up, our breathing gets shallow, and our prefrontal cortex—the part of our brains that helps us manage our emotions and impulses, plan ahead, and think clearly and flexibly—goes offline, right when we need it most. Instead, our amygdala—the distracted, reactive toddler in the back of our brain—starts running the show and all it cares about is avoiding threats and danger. And so our minds start obsessively scrolling through the past for any memories that might help us figure out what to do and projecting into the future trying to anticipate everything that could go wrong.

Despite our meat computer's best attempt to be helpful, our thinking goes off the rails. Before we even realize what's happening, a day at the beach has become a chance to rectify (or not) our previous parenting errors and a chance to prevent (or not) future problems and complications. The underlying message of that sort of thinking is that something is wrong and you have to fix it, and if you don't (which you almost certainly won't, because parenting is chaos), it's because you're a failure as a parent.

And you thought the worst thing about the beach was getting sand everywhere.

Fortunately, we always have another option. We can slow down and bring our prefrontal cortexes online just long enough to notice what's happening. Each time we do that, we give ourselves an opportunity to hop off the freak-out express, remember that chaos is normal, and do what it takes to get back on solid ground. Compassion deactivates our threat system and activates our attachment system, which decreases the stress hormones and increases our oxytocin (the hormone of trust and safety). Not surprisingly, the calmer and safer we feel, the easier it is to manage even the most screwed up moments.

No matter what's going on, chaos is just part of the deal when it comes to life with kids, so stop freaking blaming yourself for it. Whenever it feels like your life and your family and your job are out of control and you feel like you're the one screwing it all up, just remember that CHAOS stands for Compassion Helps Alleviate Our Suffering.

In a nutshell, compassion helps us clear out the mental crap, the blame, shame, anxiety, and pre-worry, so we can put away the crap map and pull out a better one, one that will help us calm down, think clearly and creatively, and move forward with confidence.

Dang. That's a pretty big nutshell.

Life just feels easier and more manageable when we know that no matter how scary or stressful things get, we'll always have at least one person on our side, reminding us that we're not alone, that life with kids is hard for everyone, and that we have the skills and strategies to manage the chaos and recover from our missteps. There are four specific parenting benefits you and your children will experience once you start tending and befriending yourself—and helpfully, they all start with C.

The Four C's: Calm, Clarity, Creativity, and Confidence

Calm

As anyone who has ever worked for a shouty boss or lived with an abusive parent or paid attention to the constant barrage of judgment and criticism happening in their own minds knows, that shit is stressful. It's incredibly distracting (because who can focus when you're constantly being reminded of how terrible everything is and/or all the ways you've made it all worse??) and the minute our fight or flight reaction is triggered, we're at high risk of becoming that shouty, abusive, critical person we so don't want to be. But when we can remember that chaos isn't a bad thing (regardless of how it feels) and that we're not actually in the running for The Shittiest Parent Ever award, we come down off high alert and shift into tend and befriend pretty quickly. When we remember we have the skills and strategies of connection, curiosity, and kindness (which you might not actually have yet, but you will by the end of this book), we calm down quickly.

Clarity

Once you calm down and let go of the contempt and criticism, you'll be able to see your situation a lot more clearly. Your vision will no longer be blurred by your regret about the past, anxiety about the future, and confusion about, well, everything. Take the Beach Day dilemma, for example. When you're able to calm down and get clear on what's actually going on, you might realize that:

A) The decision about whether or not to go to the beach in the hot, hazy weather is in fact a legitimately hard situation—and not just for you, but for everyone—and,

B) There may not be a perfect or even great solution. Again, that's not because you haven't tried hard enough or worked hard enough to find or create one, but because the perfect outcome literally doesn't exist, and,

C) The choice you make today will not, in fact, determine the fate of your relationship with your child or their future, and/or

D) You have no freaking clue what to do and you need help, or

E) You may, in fact, have another option for the day that you hadn't yet considered, which brings us to the next benefit of self-compassion.

Creativity

I don't know anyone who can think creatively or originally when it feels like everything is going to hell or they're certain they're going to make a complete mess of the whole thing. But when you're dealing with an already complicated situation and then you throw in all the quirks and preferences and particularities of each member of your family, there are no cookie-cutter solutions. You have to think creatively. Like the mom who put up cardboard dividers between her toddlers' car seats to keep them from fighting in the backseat. Or the dad who ran weekend getting-ready-for-school drills with his kids to help them practice packing their backpacks and putting on their shoes. Or the parent who got her kids to eat their veggies by turning dinner into a Crunch Contest, and the one who helped her daughter deal with nightmares by creating a Dream Jar filled with strips of paper with sweet dream ideas. These instances of parental creativity are so unique to each family and each moment that they can't be taught. But the calmer we get and the more clearly we can see the situation, the more likely it is that we'll be able to come up with a creative solution.

Confidence

One of the most insidious effects of our pervasive self-contempt is self-doubt. Regardless of what triggered it, once we end up in a spiral of shame and guilt, it becomes nearly impossible to trust ourselves. Figuring out whether or not to go to the damn beach or how to react when our kid lies to us or when to have them tested for a disability is hard enough even when we're not trying to navigate it all with a map that says, "Are you sure? I mean, you totally boffed everything last time, so what makes you think you're not going to blow it again?"

The more often we're able to respond to the snafus of life with compassion the more confident we'll feel in our own parenting abilities. To be clear, this is in no way a guarantee that you'll never make another mistake or things will never go wrong again. Of course not. Those first arrows are inevitable. But when you know that there won't be any more sharp-ass second arrows flying your way, you'll feel way more certain of yourself and your ability to take on the next challenge.

How Our Self-Compassion Helps Our Kids

Our self-compassion practice will benefit our children in a variety of ways. When we're not all tense and twisted up in all the shit that's going on and how badly we're handling it, we have a much better shot at staying present and patient with our kids, regardless of how many first arrows parenting hurls at us. When we can stay calm and respond creatively and confidently to the inevitable snafus and power struggles, we decrease the levels of conflict and tension in the family. Parenting feels easier and smoother, and we'll all be far less likely to end up in a freak-out and the subsequent shame and blame.

So that's awesome.

But wait! There's more! Imagine that contempt and compassion were languages instead of practices. Most of us adults didn't grow up speaking the language of compassion, primarily because we were raised by folks who also never learned it themselves. Self-compassion may always feel like a second language to most of us. We'll always speak it with a bit of an accent, and when we're tired or stressed we might struggle to find the right words. But it doesn't have to be that way for our kids. Rather than raising them to speak self-contempt every time the first arrows start flying, we can teach them to connect, get curious, and treat themselves with kindness.

Compassion can become our children's native language, their default response. Each time they struggle or suffer or are struck with the first arrows of life, they can learn how to stay calm, think clearly, and move forward confidently. But just like learning an actual language, this won't happen overnight. There will be plenty of freak-outs and flying shoes along the way. And when that happens, all we can do is continue to have compassion for ourselves and how damn hard parenting can be. And our kids will see that; they'll see how we treat ourselves with kindness, and over time, they'll start doing the same for themselves.

The Most Important Thing to Remember: Self-compassion isn't about letting yourself off the hook. It's an incredibly empowering practice that will help you calm down, think clearly, and approach parenting with more creativity and confidence.

CHAPTER FOUR

It All Starts with Noticing

"My life is a freaking circus."

We parents love a good circus metaphor, and it's easy to see why. Circuses are sticky and stinky and filled with animals you're pretty sure you didn't agree to. Sadly, we rarely get to relax and watch the plates spin without having to worry about who's going to clean up the mess when it all comes crashing down. Nope. We're too busy keeping track of the trapeze artists and tightrope walkers, making sure the safety nets and sparkly costumes don't have any holes, and getting all the clowns in the car when it's time to go.

I actually don't love the circus/ringmaster metaphor for two reasons: 1) It reinforces the idea that parenting is performative (which wouldn't be so bad if we could actually sell tickets and make a little money off the deal, but apparently that's frowned upon), and 2) it implies that we need to be in control of the chaos at every moment.

And you know how I feel about trying to control all that first-arrow bedlam.

Even so, most of us get so caught up in trying to control the chaos in our lives that we don't even notice the circus in our brains. I'm talking about the monkeys in our minds that start flinging second-arrow crap the minute the show goes off the rails. A good ringmaster, a good parent, they tell us, would be running a better show.

But here's the thing: Contrary to popular belief, ringmasters aren't there to make sure that every act goes perfectly smoothly. If that were true, they would spend the entire performance running around, tightening the ropes, reminding the juggling unicyclist to stay focused, and spotting the flying acrobats. The audience would be so busy watching the ringmaster scurry from place to place that not only would the entire thing seem like a shitshow (regardless of whether it actually was), but many of the best performances might go completely unnoticed.

That's why it's not the ringmaster's job to worry about every last detail. Rather, they're there for two entirely different reasons. First, to excite the crowd and build drama. Our brains are already damn good—often too good—at that.

So we're going to focus on the ringmaster's *other* job, which is to direct the audience's attention to various parts of the arena. The ringmaster is there to keep guests focused on each performance and not get distracted by the transitions between acts, the equipment moving in and out, and any falls, fails, or mistakes that will inevitably happen.

Circus performers know that failure is always a possibility; that's why they have safety nets. Despite all their practice, experience, and expertise, sometimes performers still end up in the net. They don't expect to be perfect, and neither should we. We all need a good safety net, and yes, I am absolutely talking about self-compassion.

In order to do all of that, the ringmaster has to keep an eye on each act and the overall progress of the performance, but not get sucked in by any of it. They need to be aware of what's happening all around them, but they also need to maintain enough distance and perspective on the whole situation to stay calm and make an intentional decision about what to do next.

That is *exactly* the relationship I want you to have with your own thoughts. The ability to notice when your mind-monkeys start flinging second-arrow crap—without getting caught up in it—is a first and crucial step toward practicing self-compassion. You're never going to completely get rid of your mental tendencies toward isolation, judgment, and contempt. That's the equivalent of running a perfect circus, and it's just not gonna happen. It's just not how our brains work, and that's OK! Rather, the goal is to put on your ringmaster hat as often as possible and *notice* the drama in your mind, rather than getting sucked into it.

Noticing may seem like a subtle shift in your perspective, but it's incredibly powerful and empowering in the following ways:

- Getting some distance from the chaos helps us remember that we're not responsible for everything that happens in our lives and our children's lives. Yes, we need to support, educate, and encourage the clowns we're raising, but that's not the same as controlling their every decision and behavior. Assuming we should be able to control the uncontrollable puts us at high risk of Shitty Parent Syndrome.

- When we're swept up in the mess and mayhem, we miss the beautiful, astounding, delightful moments, the ones that remind us that maybe we're not totally screwing up this whole parenting gig after all.

- Finally, if we're so distracted by the loud noises and flashing lights in our own minds, we won't have enough headspace to even realize that we're suffering or struggling. When that happens, we can't make a choice to walk away from those shit-slinging monkeys and treat ourselves with compassion instead.

Noticing is a crucial step in the practice of compassion, so we're going to dig deep into it in this chapter. We're going to get clear on exactly what noticing is, why it can be so hard to know how and what to notice, and how to practice noticing.

Why It Can Be So Damn Hard to Notice

The crazy thing about our brains is that although they notice all the time, they're not very good at noticing in intentional, consistent, or helpful ways. We might pause in the middle of a bedtime power struggle long enough to realize that everyone is far too exhausted to think clearly and the only reasonable option is to put the kid to bed and pray they've forgotten whatever it is they're upset about by morning, or we might not. We might suddenly notice that our big toe is throbbing and that pain might be the reason we've been so damn cranky, or we might not. We might realize we forgot to reschedule a meeting or text a friend and we take care of whatever it is just in time, or we might not.

That kind of noticing is great when it happens; it helps us take care of ourselves and our kids and stay on top of our shit. The problem is that it can be so random and unpredictable; we never know when we're going to keep sleepwalking through our day and when we're going to wake up at a crucial moment. Sometimes we notice that our coffee is sitting on top of the car before we drive away and sometimes we end up with coffee all over the windshield.

Our brains aren't great at noticing for a few reasons. First, they didn't evolve to slow down, step back, and take a pause from their endless ramblings. Rather, they evolved to quickly scan our surroundings, latch on to the shiny thing in the corner, anticipate what might happen next, remember the past, and react as quickly and instinctively as possible to whatever pops up—regardless of whether or not that reaction is helpful. Once our brains get going, they don't give two hoots about second arrows or crap maps or any of it.

It's not just evolution at play; we're also dealing with the challenges of modern society. We've always been prone to doing more than one thing at a time, but as screens, smartwatches, and social media have hijacked our poor little meat-computer brains, we've become masters of multitasking. And the harsh reality is that the more balls we've got in the air, the harder it is to take our eyes off them, notice how chaotic things are, and get a little perspective on the big picture. We can't be the acrobat and the ringmaster at the same time. It's just not possible.

But we keep trying to juggle everything, without noticing how distracted we are. We don't even realize that our awareness is being yanked between screaming kids, nagging notifications, irrelevant memories, relentless worries, and random thoughts about tasks we need to finish or books we want to read or that mean girl from junior high (what the hell happened to her anyway?). And then we wonder why we're so tense and exhausted at the end of the day.

Or maybe it's just that those damned first arrows keep coming at us so hard and fast that we're in a near constant state of fight or flight, which hits the gas on our survival-focused limbic system and puts the brakes on our prefrontal cortexes. The very part of our brain responsible for noticing is no longer available to us when we need it most.

Speaking of all those first arrows: Sometimes the problem is just that everything sucks, and who wants to notice that shit? Whether it's a screaming child, another horrifying headline, or our own tortured thoughts, we just don't want a front row seat to that particular circus. So we pull out our third arrows and do our best to avoid and distract ourselves from painful or intolerable thoughts and feelings. And when those thoughts and feelings manage to worm their way into our awareness, as they inevitably will, we react or run away as fast as we can (flight) without ever registering how any of it is impacting our mood, stress levels, energy, sleep, and general ability to function in the world without feeling like we're losing our minds. Basically, we keep getting caught up in all the lights and music and drama of our own brains because it never occurred to us that we have an inner ringmaster we can call on to help us figure out what to focus on, what to let go of, and what to do next.

And that's where the power of self-compassion comes into play. Self-compassion isn't about resorting to random platitudes that can feel thin and useless in the face of the very real, very sharp arrows of our lives. Rather, it's about noticing when we've been struck and choosing to take care of ourselves. Knowing that we have specific skills and strategies to respond to our own pain—no matter how bad it gets—makes everything seem a whole lot less scary.

And it all starts with noticing.

How, Exactly, to Notice

Noticing is about becoming aware of what you're doing or thinking or feeling as you're doing or thinking or feeling it. The goal is to step off the spinning carousel in your head so you can get a little perspective on what's actually happening. It's about remembering that all those thoughts, memories, and worries aren't any more reality than a circus performance is, and we can choose how much time and energy we want to invest in any of them.

Noticing happens in that instant when we shift into ringmaster mode, aware of the chaos but not consumed by it, able to choose what we want and need to focus on. The minute you start worrying about or arguing with your own thoughts or memories and anticipations, you're no longer noticing. You've just gotten caught up in yet another act, and chances are it's not a helpful one. Do your best not to judge yourself, and if you do pull out your crap map yet again, don't stress about it. Just notice it. You can't put it away if you don't even realize you're holding on to it.

There's a handy dandy acronym that mindfulness folks love that can help you notice: STOP.

External reminders—anything that reminds you that you can always step off the stage and watch the drama go by without getting caught up in it—can be incredibly useful. While I'm disinclined to suggest anything that draws you back into your phone, many meditation apps do include random or programmable timers that can trigger noticing. Other options include beaded bracelets, smooth stones you can keep in your pocket, or quotes, prayers, or photographs in notebooks, planners, or wallets—anything that can get you out of your brain and trigger you to notice.

1. Stop whatever you're doing. Just take a moment and put a pin in it. Whatever you're thinking or doing or stressing about, you can come back to it later—if you need and want to—but for now, just set it down.

2. Take a breath. Take a slow breath or a deep breath or just take a few moments to count your breaths. Even just a minute—one tiny, little, short minute—will calm you down enough so you can get a little perspective.

3. Observe. This is the noticing and curiosity part. What are you thinking? Feeling? Doing? What do you have on your plate? What are your kids doing? What do you all need? As you ask yourself these questions, try not to pull out your crap map or judge your answers. Just notice what you come up with and try to take your answers seriously.

4. Proceed. Hopefully by now you'll be calm enough to move forward with a little more clarity and intention. Remember, you just need to take the next step. That's all.

What to Notice

Every time the ringmaster steps into the middle of the big tent, they have to decide a) what to notice and b) how to respond to what they notice. Compassion is a super powerful response, and we'll get to it. But for now, we're going to focus on *what* to notice. My guess is that most ringmasters don't spend a whole lot of time worried about the pile of horse dung in the corner or the vendor selling cotton candy. They're focused on the main acts, the performers, and the staff that are going to give them useful information about what to say or do next in order to keep the show running as smoothly as possible.

Ultimately, the goal is to notice not just the first arrows, but our reactions to them, including any second arrows of contempt and third arrows of denial and distraction. If you want to dive in and start noticing those right away, you certainly can, but it can also be helpful to start practicing noticing on less stressful, more concrete experiences. I recommend starting with the present moment—your thoughts, bodily sensations, and feelings. And, of course, the more often you direct your awareness to each of these, the more likely it will be that you'll notice when shit is going down and you're blaming yourself.

Notice the Present Moment

Anything happening in the here and now is a great place to start. It will get you some much-needed space from painful memories, anxious thoughts about the future, or brutal self-contempt. Your five senses are always available to you. Wherever you are, whatever you're doing, you can take a moment to take a breath and just tune in to whatever's going on around you. Each time you intentionally direct your attention toward anything you can see, hear, touch, taste, or smell, you're practicing noticing. It's entirely possible that whatever you notice will be entirely uninteresting, boring, or, if you happen to be changing your child's diaper or driving around a bunch of ripe soccer players after a rough game, downright unpleasant, and that's OK. This isn't about entertainment or feeling good, folks. It's just about noticing.

Notice Your Thoughts

Shitty self-talk is one of the most common ways in which we abuse, harass, and undermine ourselves. It's that damn ticker tape in our minds, the one with the constant commentary, the unfavorable comparisons, and the relentless criticism. Sometimes our self-deprecating thoughts are super obvious; they're some version of "I'm such a shitty parent." But other times our self-contempt can be sneakier and more insidious; it's the deep self-doubt that we might not even be aware of but can nonetheless leave us feeling confused, incapable, and out of control.

Most folks assume that our relentless inner monologues are reasonable, logical stories and assessments of whatever is going on. Sometimes they are, and sometimes they're not. Sometimes in a moment of blessed insight we realize that our kid's current meltdown is because they're anxious about their first sleepover and not because we've raised an antisocial jerk. But other times our thoughts are more like those obnoxious pop-up boxes that blast into the middle of our computer screen, warning us of dangers that aren't real and selling us solutions we don't need. Warning! Your child is freaking out over a sleepover and therefore will never have a best friend and will wander through life lost and alone for all eternity. Your kiddo's very happiness depends on your ability to make this sleepover a complete success, so FIX IT NOW.

The bottom line is that not all thoughts are created equal. The more stressed, exhausted, overwhelmed, or emotional we are, the less helpful our thoughts are likely to be. And that's OK. I mean, it can be obnoxious and super unhelpful, but whatever. We're parents. We deal with obnoxious and unhelpful every single minute of the day. We got this.

I've said this before and I'm going to say it again: Your thoughts aren't necessarily reality, they aren't necessarily true, and while you can influence them, you definitely can't control them. And so you move through your day at the mercy of all the crap your mind-monkeys continue to fling. Or at least, you did.

But now you know that you have another option. You can choose to notice when you've gotten all wrapped up in the monkey drama—in the BS song-and-dance about how your kid is the only one who spends every afternoon playing video games instead of building robots or winning volleyball tournaments. And you can decide to remind yourself that parenting is hard, that not every child is a robot and volleyball superstar, and that your kid came home with an A on their science test. You'll likely need to notice and redirect your attention over and over again (those monkeys can be relentless!), but that's OK. It doesn't mean you're doing anything wrong, it's just another opportunity to practice noticing.

Notice Your Feelings

We all know what feelings are: joy, sadness, fear, surprise, rage, guilt, etc. Sometimes we know what triggers our feelings; we feel happy, confident, and proud when we get a promotion at work, or our kid finally learns how to read after months of tutoring. Or maybe we feel heartbroken and pissed because our marriage is falling apart, or we got another call from the school about something inappropriate our kid did in the middle of class. And sometimes we have no freaking clue why we feel the way we do; everything can seem completely fine and suddenly we feel like crap. It happens to all of us.

Folks have wildly different experiences of, and relationships to, their feelings. Some of us feel them quite intensely and easily, and some of us barely register them at all. Some of us know when we're having a feeling and are pretty good at identifying what that feeling is, and others could use a little (or a lot of) help in this particular arena. Wherever you fall on the spectrum of knowing how to feel your feelings, there are a few things to keep in mind:

Feelings aren't wrong. Seriously. Your feelings are never wrong for what you're thinking. They might be incredibly unpleasant or annoying or confusing, but they're not wrong, and you don't have to apologize for how you feel. This can be a tough pill to swallow, especially after a lifetime of being told or treated otherwise, but it's true. (Of note: This is also true for your kids, and it can be useful to remember the difference between feelings and behaviors. It is absolutely acceptable for your son to be pissed at your daughter, and it's totally, totally fine for you to be just as mad at your son. But it's not OK for any of you to start throwing your shoes at each other.)

Every feeling has a beginning, a middle, and an end. We often don't even realize we're having a feeling until we're caught up in the worst of it and it feels like it will never end. We

The best metaphor I've ever come across for making sense of our feelings is the weather. Lots of folks assume that their big, unpleasant feelings are like catastrophic storms that will destroy their lives, so they do whatever it takes to avoid, avoid, avoid. Fortunately, that's not how feelings work; they're more like typical weather. Sometimes we wake up to a sunny day, sometimes it's just a bit overcast, and sometimes the storm is raging. Sometimes we can predict when the storm will roll in, and sometimes the temperature drops and crap starts falling out of the sky for no clear reason. No matter what we're feeling or what the weather is, what matters is that a) it's not our fault, b) we can't control it, and c) it will pass. It might rain for a week, but eventually it will pass.

can be drowning in emotional overwhelm, but each time we can get enough space to realize that we're having a feeling, it's as though we got our heads above water just long enough to take a breath. We might get pulled back under, and that's OK. The goal is to just keep noticing and breathing until we make it back to solid ground.

We can't control our feelings, but we can influence them. Sad songs, scary movies, and upsetting news headlines can, and do, mess with our moods. Alternately, getting enough sleep, exercising regularly, drinking the perfect amount of coffee, spending time with loved ones, listening to our favorite song, watching a hilarious video, and learning how to not take our kid's shenanigans personally can all help us feel better in tough moments. And sometimes we do everything right and we still feel like shit. What can I say? It happens. Either way, we can't make a choice to take care of our feelings if we don't even realize we're having them in the first place.

Notice Your Bodily Sensations

We parents tend to live in our heads. We're constantly worrying and planning and reacting and fixing and solving problems that may or may not have actually happened yet, so we don't even notice what's going on with our bodies until the baby yanks our hair or our kiddo accidentally headbutts us in the chin. But whether we're in physical pain or emotional pain, our bodies are important sources of information about our feelings and functioning.

Sometimes our bodily sensations are clear and straightforward; our neck and shoulders are rock hard because we've just spent six hours hunched over a computer and that might explain why we're so damn irritable. Sometimes our discomfort or pain is a symptom of something bigger—an undiagnosed allergy or chronically overwhelming stress—that we just don't have the time or energy to deal with.

And sometimes our bodily sensations are trying to tell us that we're having a feeling. Thoughts hang out in our heads, but feelings take up residence in our stiff shoulders, twisted up bellies, and aching temples. Love can leave us feeling warm all over, while sadness feels heavy in our chest. Our breathing gets shallow and fast when we're anxious, and our muscles tense up when we're angry. And sometimes the best thing we can do when we're neck-deep in shitty feelings is tune into, and take care of, our bodies. This is absolutely a form of self-compassion. Every time we ignore or dismiss the tension, tightness, butterflies, or bruising in our bodies, we might as well be stumbling around in the dark. When we realize we're hungry, exhausted, confused, or in pain, we can flip on the light, stop beating ourselves up, and choose to take care of ourselves instead.

Notice Your Freak-outs: Fight, Flight, Freeze, Freak Out, Fix, and Fawn

These are some of the hardest behaviors to notice, because by the time we're flipping out, our prefrontal cortexes (the noticing parts of our brains) are offline, and our limbic systems (the unpredictable, reactive toddlers) are running the show. Yikes.

Having said that, it is absolutely possible to notice our freak-outs. We can notice the tension rising in our bodies, our angry, confused, anxious, or sad feelings brewing, and our thoughts exploding. And yes, we can absolutely notice when we're screaming at our kids, attempting to bribe them into better behavior or scrambling to fix their shitty feelings. And when—not if, but when—everything feels out of control and you have no idea which arrows are first arrows and which arrows are second and third arrows and what's a thought and what's a feeling, go back to basics. Notice your breathing. Put your hands flat on the counter and notice the sensations of the cool surface under your fingers. That will calm you down enough to figure out what to notice next.

How to Practice Noticing

The good news is that noticing is a skill, something we can get better at with practice. The more we practice, the more we'll find ourselves not only noticing the first arrows in consistent, intentional, and super helpful ways, but we'll also be more likely to notice the beautiful and sweet moments. Ignoring or overlooking the joys and successes of our lives is another sign of our self-contempt, while tuning into the positive moments can make our lives feel easier and less stressful. Whether it's a child's first somersault, their first A in chemistry, or just a kid spontaneously saying thank you, all of those wins and sweet moments make life feel just a little better and a little easier. And even a little easier is a big deal in a world that feels like it's just one challenge after another.

So, as you start your noticing practice, there are a few ideas to keep in mind:

First, **it's easier to practice when it's easy**. As John F. Kennedy so aptly noted, "The time to repair the roof is when the sun is shining." If you're not sure what to notice or how to notice it, don't jump right into the most brutal or painful aspects of your experience. Just try to notice the pleasant stuff, the benign moments, or the only slightly shitty situations; all of that will help you build up the skills and strategies you'll need in the roughest moments. You can also choose one or two things you do every day—drinking your coffee, walking back from the bus stop, snuggling your kiddo in bed at night—and do your best to notice when your thoughts wander and try to just keep noticing what you're doing.

Whatever you do, **don't go making this into something bigger than it is.** You don't need to turn yourself into a yogi or start meditating for an hour every day (although either of those would be totally awesome if you can swing it). This is just about a slight shift in your awareness. That's all.

Next, **remember that you're always practicing something**, whether or not it's something you actually want to get better at. So many of you have spent years studying your crap map, ruminating on all the ways you think you're screwing up, failing your kids, or not meeting your own expectations, that you've gotten really damn good at it. So now it's time to start practicing *noticing* when you've pulled out the crap map so you can toss it and pick a new one.

Noticing something doesn't mean that you're OK with it, whatever "it" is. It doesn't mean that you're not going to challenge or change it. It just means that it's there, you're aware it's there—and, not to make your head spin any faster than it already is, you're aware of your awareness. In addition, your noticing isn't going to increase or intensify whatever is going on. In fact, it's just the opposite. When you shift from "I'm so freaking sick of dealing with my freaking kids" to "I'm having the thought that I'm so freaking sick of my freaking kids," that thought loses some of its power and intensity. You realize it's not your reality and it doesn't define you as a parent; it's just another thought passing across your consciousness, and you can decide whether you want to keep dancing with it or if you want to step off the dance floor. This is especially important to keep in mind if what you're noticing is particularly unpleasant, scary, or painful. You can absolutely become aware of something without being defined by it.

Singletasking, or doing just one thing at a time, is important for any practice, and it's crucial for noticing. Any time we're trying to pay attention to multiple tasks, thoughts, or transitions at once, we're far more likely to screw up at least one of them. As much as we'd like to believe otherwise, our meat-computer minds just aren't great at multitasking. Multitasking stresses us out, slows us down, and makes it far more likely that we'll screw something up. The more we can focus on doing just one thing at a time, the more we can get our brains and bodies on the same page, the calmer we'll feel, and the more effective and efficient our practicing will be.

Just like anything else you practice, **your noticing practice is dose-dependent**. The more often you become aware of your own thoughts, feelings, and experiences, the more you reap the benefits of that awareness. It might be a particularly bumpy road at first, because most of you have no idea how incredibly rough you're being on yourselves. In fact, it can be a bit overwhelming to realize how often you're sending those shitty parent texts, both in our own mind and to your friends. It really does gets better with practice.

How Our Noticing Benefits Our Children

Every single one of the practices in this book will benefit your children both directly and indirectly. And even though our noticing practice is a deeply internal experience and often just a small shift in perspective, it can be incredibly powerful and beneficial for our kiddos nonetheless.

On a super concrete level, we'll be more likely to notice when our kids' basic needs are going unmet. It's hard to miss a kid doing a pee-pee dance or screaming for a cookie, but sometimes our children aren't great at expressing their needs quite so clearly (*cough* understatement of the year *cough*). When we get better at not getting sucked into the drama of their truly terrible one-man show, we'll be more likely to realize that the reason our kids are being so obnoxious, argumentative, or uncooperative is not because they hate us and want to make our lives miserable, but because they're hungry, exhausted, or in pain. And when we realize that, we can feed, soothe, or put them to bed. That doesn't always solve the problem, but it can sidestep a major power struggle more often than not.

On a more indirect level, the more consistently we can become aware of all the first arrows flying right at us, the more consistently we'll treat ourselves compassionately. And when we're not being hit with second and third arrows all the time, we'll be less distracted, wounded, and overwhelmed by the pain of self-contempt. As parenting feels easier and less stressful, we'll be more flexible and less rigid and reactive, which is definitely a huge benefit for our children.

Advanced Noticing Practice

Almost every parent I know has either a) started a meditation practice, b) thought about starting a meditation practice, or c) refused to even consider a meditation practice because who has time for that navel-gazing baloney when the dishwasher needs to be unloaded? But basic mindfulness meditation has nothing to do with navel gazing or clearing our minds or aligning our chakras or whatever. It's just a noticing practice. You pick something to focus your attention on—often your breathing—and every time your mind wanders (which it will, usually before you even get to your second inhale), you just notice that it wandered and come back to your breathing.

Mindfulness meditation doesn't just strengthen the noticing neurons in our minds; it's also a great way to get to know our own style of self-contempt and our preferred freak-outs. When we push pause on the distractions and task lists and dirty laundry of our lives, all we have left to notice are our thoughts, feelings, and bodily sensations. And for all the reasons we explored in Chapter 1, those thoughts and feelings are rarely focused on what awesome parents we are, how we're totally on top of our shit, and how nice it is to just chill and breathe for a few minutes. Rather, we end up in a spiral of everything we've screwed up, everything we need to fix, and shit, we forgot to email the school counselor. But each time we notice those thoughts and choose not to leap into action but rather to stay focused on our breathing, we're practicing something really important. And the next time we're in the middle of chaos, we'll be more likely to notice when we're itching for a fight, freezing up, or flipping out. And once we've noticed that, we're no longer at the mercy of our own instincts. We can choose what to focus on next.

The Most Important Thing to Remember: Noticing is often just a tiny shift in perspective, but it will completely change your relationship to, and ability to manage, whatever is going on.

CHAPTER FIVE

You're Not the Only One: The Power of Connection

Let's go back to the Beach Day scenario of Chapter 2. Imagine that right in the middle of the morning chaos, just as your partner was skulking in the kitchen, your daughter was slamming her bedroom door, and you were hiding in the bathroom, the doorbell rang. It's a good friend from down the street, and she's here to give you some blueberry muffins from a batch she just whipped up.

She must see the tension on your face because she asks how you're doing. You pause for a moment and consider the situation. Not only does your friend have her shit together enough to bake something yummy, but she was thoughtful (and organized) enough to bring some to you and your family. As if that wasn't enough, it looks like she's already showered and she's definitely brushed her hair.

Gah.

If you didn't like her so much, you'd probably despise her.

Meanwhile, you and your family can't even decide whether or not to even leave the house (much less actually do it) without a massive meltdown. And so you stand there in the doorway like a complete idiot, staring at the muffins and trying to figure out how to answer her seemingly innocent question about how you are. What the hell are you supposed to say?

Why It Can Be So Damn Hard to Connect and Feel Connected

If that had been me answering the door to Happy Muffin Mom in my early years of parenting, I would have smiled and nodded and told her we were getting ready to head out for a day at the beach. This was totally not true, of course, but back then there was no way in hell I was going to 'fess up to our mess. I was absolutely certain that if I told the truth, her response would inevitably confirm what I already knew: that Beach Days just weren't a problem for her and her family.

I spent the first several years of motherhood really and truly believing that I was the only parent who dreaded picking my girls up from daycare and preschool because I had no idea if I was going to get my sweet little snugglebuns or some crazy-ass hell-beasts whose heads might spin around at any moment. I was pretty damn sure I was the only mother who was actively teaching my twenty-month-old how to watch TV because I could not, for the life of me, figure out any other way to handle bedtime with a newborn and a toddler on my own. And I was certain that somehow every other parent had figured out how to balance parenting and work and I was the only one who felt completely confused about my career, and if I still even had one or wanted one and oh shit the girls just spilled an entire container of fuse beads on the kitchen floor so excuse me while I go cry in the corner.

I mean, I guess I sorta kinda knew on some intellectual level that parenting was rough for everyone and there was no such thing as a perfect parent, but only in the same way I knew Greenland existed. I've never been to Greenland and I don't know anyone who's ever been there and, if I'm being super honest, I have no reason to believe that Greenland is anything more than a blur on the map on the wall in our kitchen. And I was pretty damn certain that if I ever did make it to Greenland, it would be full of more Happy Muffin Moms.

Of course it would.

This belief that we are somehow different from and worse than other parents is such a painfully sharp arrow. The sense that we're failing our children is a nearly constant companion for some of us. And some of us have plenty of good days, or even months, before our child makes some developmental leap or starts middle school or our anxiety spikes and all of a sudden we're in over our heads again. Either way, each time our Shitty Parent Syndrome flares up, and shame clouds our thinking, making it hard to get clear on what's actually happening and feel confident about what to do next.

In addition, each time we isolate—physically, emotionally, and/or psychologically—in times of crisis, or even just the normal chaos, we're disconnecting ourselves not only from our support system—from the people we need the most when arrows start flying—but also from the reality checks that are such a crucial part of our compassion practice. This deeply human tendency to hide the truth and only share the best of ourselves not only makes life and parenting harder, but it also reinforces our deep-seated and deeply untrue thoughts, beliefs, and perceptions that we suck way worse than other parents. And the more we believe we suck more than everyone else, the less likely we are to reach out in times of need. The less often we reach out when we need help, the more likely we are to believe that no one else struggles like we do. It's a super shitty self-reinforcing cycle of disconnection.

So why the hell do we do this to ourselves?

The short story is that we don't. Not really.

This may seem super weird seeing as how you are, in fact, the one who's either choosing to connect or reach out or not. But there are actually a ton of social structures and societal norms that leave us isolated, confused, and far more likely to compare our internal experiences to everyone else's external presentation. Let's explore just a few of them.

The Air-conditioning Effect. Before air-conditioning was invented, we all kept our windows open, which meant we could hear everything that was going in the neighborhood, including when the parents next door were losing their shit with their kids or their spouses or their dogs or whatever. And while I'm fairly certain that none of us miss long summer days of sweating profusely, all those closed windows mean we no longer know what's going on behind our neighbor's closed doors. The only meltdowns we hear are our own, which further perpetuates our belief that we're the only ones who aren't always patient, calm, and kind at every moment.

Fewer Free-Range Kids. Back in the good old days when everyone was sweating and yelling loud enough for the whole neighborhood to hear, it was far more likely that one parent was working and the other one (almost always the mom) was home with the kids. Moms at home had more time to connect with other mothers, to share their stories and struggles. And when the kids came home from school and bounced from house to house in search of cookies and Kool-Aid, the at-home parents heard their stories, and I know I don't need to tell you that kids don't hide the truth.

As more and more parents are working, more moms and dads are racing from drop-off to work to pick-up and then home for the end-of-the-day grind. We move through our days in a silo of stress, with few, if any, opportunities to connect with other parents, share our stories, and hear theirs. Now, I'm not suggesting that we go back to the days of rigid gender norms and women who had no real choice but to stay at home, but it's useful to be aware of the side effects of this cultural shift.

Mouthy Parenting Experts. Don't get me wrong; I love good parenting advice as much as the next guy. And my family and I have benefited from that advice, so much so that I felt compelled to dole out a bit of my own. But if that advice isn't served up with a healthy dose of reality, honesty, and compassion, it can leave us feeling as though there's actually a right way to raise kids, but no matter how hard we try, we keep getting it wrong.

The Happiness Movement. Over the past few decades, the self-help world has become hyper-focused on happiness. It's the topic of bestselling books, popular podcasts, and in-demand college courses. Now, I have no problem with educating folks about the factors that might maybe help them be happier or even just less anxious and stressed, but at the end of the day, happiness is a feeling and we can't control how we feel any more than we can control the weather. Even so, we're left assuming that if everyone else is happy and we're not, it's not because struggling and suffering and being unhappy is an inherent part of the human experience—it's because we've done something wrong.

Stupid Social Media. And then there are all those obnoxiously perfect parents pretending like they're not even trying when they're actually spending a shitload of time setting up their seemingly spur of the moment image, which we then can't help but compare our chaotic mess of a life to. Gah.

It's like we're out there standing in the rain without an umbrella, and each time we look up, our lives and social media feeds are filled with happy, smiley parents just chomping at the bit to explain to us how they stay dry even in the midst of the craziest storm. Instead of acknowledging that it's raining and looking for an umbrella or raincoat, we're so busy wondering what the hell is wrong with us and why we're the only ones getting wet and how that's going to screw up our kids for the rest of their lives that we don't even notice that we're freezing cold and soaked to the bone. And man, it's super hard to parent well when you're wet and cold.

Connection Is the Antidote to Isolation

So now is when we get to the good stuff.

Connection.

Connection is the antidote to all the shame and self-imposed isolation that is so common in Shitty Parent Syndrome. The knowledge—the deeply held, unshakable belief—that parenting is inconvenient and confusing and unpredictable for *every single one of us* is a game changer. Don't get me wrong; this sense of connection won't get your jerk of a boss to shut up or your kids to shower without a massive meltdown, but this sense of common humanity, as compassion researcher Kristen Neff calls it, will help you feel less overwhelmed and better able to deal with whatever's going on.

The ability to remind ourselves of our common humanity is the goal, but it's not always easy, especially if we've spent years and even decades believing just the opposite. Fortunately, there are a bunch of ways to make it easier, including connecting to common humanity, trusted adults, and the present moment, and disconnecting from the people and experiences that don't serve us well. There's no one right way to do all of this, so pick the strategies that work for you. It's all good, as long as you feel less alone and more connected.

Connecting to Our Common Humanity

Common humanity is the knowledge and awareness that our chaos is what connects us to other parents, rather than separates us from them. The goal here is to shift your thinking from "I caused this shitshow; I have to fix it" or "I have one chance at this parenting gig, and I'm blowing it" to some version of:

"Yup, this seems about right for five p.m. on a school day."

"Just another snafu—we all deal with them."

"Man, tired two-year-olds are *tough*. Parenting is tough."

That's all. It's just knowing that chaos is normal and you're not alone. Super simple, extremely powerful, but not always so easy, especially when we've been telling ourselves just the opposite for years. The trick is to remind ourselves of the fundamental truth of common humanity often enough that we eventually believe it. Fortunately, there are lots of ways to get ourselves out of our crap thinking and help us remember that whatever we're dealing is part of the deal with raising humans in the twenty-first century.

The first step is to notice your second-arrow thoughts, especially the ones that leave you feeling all alone. Any time you start comparing yourself to other parents, or thinking that no other parent has been through what you're going through, or you're the only who [insert your failure, either real or perceived here], just try to notice those thoughts and not get sucked into them. This noticing will calm you down enough to bring your prefrontal cortex back online, which should help you think a little more clearly and move on to step 2.

Step 2 is to remember that your thoughts are just thoughts. They could be the cure to your current crisis or the biggest bunch of bullshit this side of the Mississippi, and the trick is to get enough distance from those thoughts to discern the difference.

This is a great time for a quick review of the difference between *judgment* and *discernment*. Judgment is about deciding one thing is better than another, that one is right and one is wrong. And that sort of judgment will trigger your Shitty Parent Syndrome in less time than it took you to read this sentence. Discernment, however, is just about noticing a difference, and making a distinction between skillful thoughts and unskillful ones. Skillful thoughts bring you closer to your goal—which in this case is your belief in common humanity—while unskillful thoughts send you deeper into isolation.

So keep on noticing and doing whatever you can to remind yourself that parenting is hard for everyone, and that scorched dinners and cranky kids and misplaced permission slips are not a YOU problem but an ALL OF US problem.

Here are some strategies for how to make this easier:

- Remember, again and again, that just as you don't have to believe every thought that crosses your mind, you can choose to think thoughts even if you're not sure that you believe them yet. You can absolutely keep reminding yourself of your connection to common humanity, even if you think it's total crap. That's totally fine. Keep repeating it and you'll get there.
- If that feels too hard, try replacing "I" with "we." The "we" is a stand-in for all of us who are collectively parenting children at this moment on Earth. Each time you find yourself thinking, "I'm a terrible parent" or "I'm screwing up my kids," just

switch it to "We're terrible parents" or "We're screwing up our kids." I promise, shit doesn't seem nearly so hard when you're part of a "we."

- If changing your thoughts, even by one word, just isn't working for you, try singing your thoughts or say them in a ridiculous accent. It's really hard to take yourself so damn seriously when you sound like Kermit the Frog. Remember, the whole goal is to not take the bait of your unhelpful thoughts. Then go back and repeat the first two steps as often as possible.
- When none of the above is working at all, it's time to call in a lifeline, aka a trusted adult.

Connecting to Trusted Adults

We social workers love to talk about "trusted adults," but for some reason we tend to reserve that phrase for children. Just like light-up sneakers and kids' menus, the phrase "trusted adults" shouldn't be just for the under-thirteen set. Grown-ups need them too. I'm talking about the friends, family members, professionals, and other people who support us, both online and in real life. This connection isn't always about asking for help and advice (although it can be), and it's not about finding our Yes Friends who will always take our side and tell us we're right and that the other person is an unmitigated dick (although sometimes that's nice to hear). In this case, I'm talking about reaching out to those folks in our lives who we know will listen to what we're going through and not judge us but will show up with curiosity, compassion, and maybe even their own hilariously horrifying stories about the time their kids also barfed over the side of the boat in the It's a Small World ride at Disney World.

So, who are these people and how do we find them? Trusted adults aren't necessarily friends (although they can be), but they can also be therapists, counselors, physicians, and members of the clergy, for example. In addition, not every friend is a trusted adult. There are lots of people that I like very much, and who I can share a good laugh with on the playground, but I know—either from experience or from that gurgle in my gut—that they're not the folks I'm going to turn to when I need reassurance or a reality check. This doesn't mean they're bad people; they might be so wounded by their own second and third arrows that they can't even imagine that they might be able to connect with anyone else around those pain points. Or maybe they're a great trusted adult for someone else, but not for you. And that's OK. Not everyone is for everyone.

Trusting someone with something doesn't mean we have to trust them with everything. We get to choose who we reach out to or open up to, what we share with them, and when we share it. It's OK to put your toe in the water, see how it feels, notice how you feel, and decide whether you want to visit that particular pond again.

Let's go back to Happy Muffin Mom and her question about how you're doing. You have a few different options for how to respond, which will result in various levels of connection or isolation:

Option A: You plaster a fake-ass smile on your face and talk about how excited you are to go to the sandcastle contest because you had such an amazing time last year and the beach is such a magical place and blah blah blah. Your friend would almost certainly smile back and nod and talk about how she and her family had such a blast at the beach last weekend and it's one of their favorite places and blah blah blah.

Despite the fact that you're not telling the truth, you totally assume she is. For all you know, she might be cringing inwardly at the memory of her last beach trip, the fights over sunscreen, the bickering over beach toys, the meltdowns over failed sandcastles or popsicles dropped in the sand. But she thinks you and your crew have picture-perfect Beach Days, which makes her feel even more ashamed of her own shitshow, so she keeps her mouth shut. And you both walk away from the interaction feeling even more isolated, even more certain that you're the only parent who can't even pull off a simple trip to the shore.

So that sucks.

Fortunately, you also have an option B, which involves some version of you telling the truth in response to the "how are you" question. This could go in a few different directions, such as:

- "I'm . . . meh. We're trying to get to the beach, and well, let's just say it's been a morning."
- "We're hoping to get to the sandcastle contest, but at this point we'll be lucky if we can get the kid out of her bedroom."
- "We'd planned to go to the beach today, but the air quality sucks and I'm worried about my daughter's asthma but she really wants to go and I have no freaking clue what to do."

- "We're trying to get to the beach but everything sucks and I'm completely overwhelmed and I was hiding in the bathroom when you rang the bell and I'm seriously considering taking these muffins and heading back in there after you leave."

How much you share likely depends on your style and how well you know and trust this friend, but even if you aren't particularly close, any version of "life isn't perfect" is going to open the door to a more authentic exchange. When we share a little bit of our reality, we're creating space for our friends to a) share some of theirs, and/or b) respond to us with kindness and compassion.

And yes, there is a point to all of this and it's not just that sharing is caring. And you're not just fishing for sympathy. Rather,

Never be scared alone. Early in my social work career, I worked on a locked inpatient psychiatric unit. I loved that job—almost all the time. But sometimes it got scary, generally when my patients or their visitors were behaving in unpredictable, threatening, or violent ways. After a particularly harrowing moment, the attending physician on my team took me aside and gave me one of the most useful pieces of advice I've ever received: "Never be scared alone." Those four words have gotten me through some of the most terrifying, confusing, and overwhelming moments of my life and parenting.

you are intentionally and authentically creating the space for the connection of compassion. This isn't about realizing you both hate the beach and love blueberry muffins (although that's cool too), it's about giving your friends (and, as we'll discuss later, yourself) the opportunity to notice, acknowledge, and respond to your suffering with curiosity and kindness. More often than not, this sort of connection will help you remember that you didn't create this current snafu, and it's OK if you can't fix it.

Connecting to the Present Moment

Sometimes, no matter how well intentioned we are, no matter how hard we're trying, the arrows are flying so hard and fast and we're so overwhelmed that we can't even remember that connection is an option. When that happens, we're at high risk of falling back into old unhelpful patterns of second-arrow thoughts of self-flagellation and shame and third-arrow behaviors.

Those moments are precisely when we need a simple, easy strategy that requires very little of our muddled meat computers. That's when we need the present moment. Letting go of our thoughts and focusing our attention on the here and now is the fastest, most effective way to calm down our freaking out toddler brain, bring our prefrontal cortex back online, and help shut down the shit talk you're flinging at yourself.

Step 1: Notice that you're in a rough spot. Maybe you're about to explode at your kids, but it could be that your dark thoughts are gathering or your anxiety is amping way up. It could just be that you're so damn tired you can barely string two words together, much less make another damn dinner. Don't judge, just notice. And if you do judge, just notice that too. Briefly curse that crazy lady who keeps nagging you about noticing, and then notice that too.

Step 2: Find something to focus on. It can be anything that actually exists in the present moment that you can experience with any of your five senses. At this stage in the process, I don't recommend focusing on your thoughts until you're calm enough to not get sucked in by them. Your breath is a great choice because it's always with you (and if it's not, you've got bigger problems than I can cover in this book). However, anything you can see, hear, touch, smell, or taste is fair game. You can count the tiles on your bathroom floor, tune in to the birds chirping or the refrigerator humming, spread your hands out flat on the counter, breathe in the aroma of your coffee or tea, or slow down and notice the flavor of the popcorn you're mindlessly shoving in your mouth.

There's no right or wrong way to do this, but some folks prefer a little more structure. If that's the case, try the 5-4-3-2-1 method, which involves noticing:

- Five things you can see
- Four things you can touch
- Three things you can hear
- Two things you can smell
- One thing you can taste

Having said that, I've been a parent long enough to know that the aromas and flavors of life with kids aren't always so pleasant, so if stinky diapers or sweaty hockey socks or day-old macaroni and cheese isn't working for you, then just stick with whatever you can see, touch, and hear.

Breathing is the fastest and most effective way to come back to the present moment. It helps focus your unruly thoughts and sends a direct message to your nervous system that you can calm down. But if focusing on your breath stresses you out for any reason, that's OK too. You have lots of other options.

Unless you're running a side gig as a Zen master, chances are that you won't even make it through noticing one breath or seeing one thing before your thinking machine gets going again and before you know it, you're flooded by worry, regret, confusion, and stress all over again. And that's OK. That's just what happens. Except for those rare moments when the present moment happens to be super exciting or engaging, your brain isn't going to be inclined to hang out there. It doesn't mean there's anything wrong with you or your thinking; it just means that after decades of shooting yourself with second arrows it can be damn hard to put down your bow. Nothing to beat yourself up about, just keep noticing and breathing and practicing. It will get easier.

Once you've calmed down and gotten a little clarity, you can go back to your other connection practices, and/or you can disconnect from the bullshit.

Disconnecting from the Bullshit

Have you ever tried tidying your house while your kids are still awake and spinning like Tasmanian devils? It's kind of like brushing your teeth while you're eating Oreos. And that's precisely what we're doing to ourselves when we keep hanging out with folks or putting ourselves in situations—both virtual and in real life—that leave us feeling disconnected, isolated, doubtful, and confused.

This could be that woman who always shows up to the newborn parent support group in a strapless sundress with a perfect blow-out (yes, I've seen it), the one whose biggest problem seems to be that her son's Advanced Latin for Tots class overlaps with her own volunteer work saving baby seals. It could be the baseball parents who blow you off at every game, the family members who constantly criticize your parenting, your book club or trivia buddies who give you just a little too much shit a little too often, or the therapist or doctor who floods you with judgment masquerading as well-intentioned advice.

You know who I'm talking about. The Perfectly Put Together Parent, The Parent Who Refuses to Acknowledge You No Matter How Many Times You've Met Them, The Overly Critical Grandparent, and the Judgmental Pediatrician.

And it's not just actual people we actually know. (Although they are often the worst, because they're just so freaking real.) Each swipe through social media images of perfect parents looking perfectly happy and perfectly pulled together seems to only magnify our own flaws and failings. And the fake news is *everywhere*. I mean, you guys, I recently watched an entire season (or three, ahem) of a reality show about a family with eighteen kids, including multiple sets of multiples and not once—NOT ONE FREAKING TIME—did either parent snap, yell, or scream. I'm sorry, WHAT? Oh, right. *It's not reality.* But no matter how often we may try to remind ourselves that all this phoney baloney has been highly edited or filtered or whatever, some part of our overworked little meat computer of a brain still falls for it.

Look, it's not about what they say or do or how they say or do it. It has nothing to do with whether or not they know what they're talking about or are completely full of shit. The only thing that matters as you scroll through social media is what you think and how you feel about yourself and your place in the world of parents each time you're in those situations.

Hopefully by now you know where we're headed: You gotta *notice* when you're triggered. The trick here, of course, is to not just notice whatever you're feeling or thinking, but to respect whatever it is you're noticing. Try not to ignore it or minimize your experience or justify or defend whoever or whatever is triggering you. Once you've gotten some space, it's time to figure out what to do next, and you have a couple of options:

Whenever possible, stop hanging out with those folks.

Set your boundaries and respect them (your boundaries, that is, not the jerks giving you side-eye). Be relentless. Sit at the other end of the bleachers, find a new bowling league, request a new pediatrician, turn off the damn reality show and turn on *The Simpsons* or *Schitt's Creek*, and please please please in the name of all things holy, stop following all those social media accounts full of parenting advice and suggestions for how to organize the perfect playroom. Unfollow with wild abandon. Fill your feed with cat memes and basketball clips or whatever makes you happy.

Just say no, unless you really really seriously want to say yes. People will make all sorts of requests of you, from volunteer opportunities to coaching and committees. These can be great opportunities to connect, but they're not necessary. Before you say yes, take the time to consider who else is on the committee, what the work is, and whether you actually have the time and energy to do it. If you think it's unlikely that you'll make a connection there, or you're not excited about the work, or it's going to leave you even more overwhelmed, exhausted, or drained, then say no. You can absolutely be kind and friendly and appropriate and all those good adulty things even as you're standing firm in your boundaries. If you're having a hard time setting limits, think of the situation as an opportunity to model what you want your kids to learn. Do you want them to feel compelled to say yes to every request that crosses their path, even if it's likely to make them feel worse or make their lives harder?

Just think no. Learning to hold your boundaries is especially important because there will always be colleagues, family members, neighbors, or teachers that you have no choice but to see from time to time. And that's just when you need to set your boundaries on the inside. You can be civil and polite and watch the big game together and collaborate on a work project, but that doesn't mean you have to open up or give these folks or their opinions any more space in your brain than they already have. This is when it's totally acceptable to answer the potentially personal questions with vague responses that aren't rude, but don't necessarily invite more conversation, such as:

"I'm fine, thanks for asking."

"It's complicated."

"That sounds like a tricky situation."

"Who knows? Anything could happen."

"Yup, all good."

"Rent-free." I learned this phrase from my sixteen-year-old nephew, and I can't stop thinking about it. Basically, no one has the right to live rent-free in your mind unless you let them. Your brain is some seriously precious real estate, so the minute you notice those squatters messing with your thoughts, feel free to kick them out. You might have to kick them out again and again, but setting those boundaries and holding them is a seriously skillful and compassionate move.

Finally, consider the advice of my favorite social worker, Brené Brown. She carries a small piece of paper in her wallet. It has the names of the folks whose opinions of her matter. As Brown puts it, "To be on that list, you have to love me for my strengths and struggles. You have to know that I'm trying to be Wholehearted, but I still cuss too much, flip people off under the steering wheel, and have both Lawrence Welk and Metallica on my iPod." Make your list and review it as often as you need to.

Trickier Situations

Remembering our common humanity is hard enough for those of us who match the dominant family narrative in our neighborhood, community, and culture. In the United States, that means white, cis, heterosexual, Christian, two-parent families with children who don't have significant or noticeable developmental delays or physical, emotional, mental health, or learning disabilities and enough money to sign those super healthy kids up for pee-wee hockey, dance lessons, and SAT tutoring. If that happens to describe your family, then you're far more likely to see yourself and your children represented in movies, books, TV shows, TikTok videos, and the covers of parenting books. That doesn't guarantee that you'll never feel alone, but it might make it easier to feel connected to common humanity when you're struggling.

However, things can get a whole lot trickier if you, your family, or your children fall outside those specific boxes. If any or all of you don't fit into what we are constantly told is the norm, if you or your family members are people of color, neurodivergent, don't speak English as your first language, are LGBTQ, or are living with any kind of disability, it may be harder to remember that you belong, and that your experience—your awesome kick-ass moments and your roughest days—are all part of life on this planet. Maybe you celebrate Hannukah or Ramadan. Maybe all of your money goes toward shelter and food. Or maybe you're a single parent who can't join the parents' social night. In these cases, it can be so much harder to connect to common humanity and so much easier to blame yourself.

But self-blame was so four chapters ago, so let's consider the other possibilities:

Be super vigilant about your boundaries. Ditch the haters. No excuses or explanations needed.

Remember that the hard stuff isn't your fault. If your experience feels super hard, it's probably because it is—and not because of anything you did. That's just what happens when you live in a world that privileges certain families' experiences over others, and you don't happen to be one of those certain families. Do whatever you can to hold on to that broader perspective. Remember that the society and culture we live in has a huge impact on our lives and how we make sense of them. It can be tough to hang on to the big picture because the details of our lives feel so damn personal, which is why connecting with other folks who share your experience and pull you out of your own chaos is so important.

Find your community. Reminding yourself that you're not alone is a great start, but it's not enough—especially when you don't often see yourself and your family reflected in pop culture or the media. A community of like-minded folks who can relate to your experience will be a powerful source of connection for you. This could be a monthly meet-up with other parents of children with cerebral palsy, an online forum for single mothers by choice, a support group for grieving parents, or a religious community that's explicitly welcoming to LGBTQ families. Whenever possible, try to find opportunities to get together in person; while virtual connections are better than nothing, they're not the same as live interactions. This might take some work, and you might have to ask around or try out a few different communities (assuming they're available) before you find the one that's the right match for you, but hang in there. It's worth it.

Find a different community. If you live in a rural area or you or your partner are constantly moving (perhaps because you're in the military or your job demands it), well, good luck with everything I just said. This isn't a diss on small towns; it's just that statistically speaking, fewer people overall means fewer people like you and your family. If that's the case, you have two other options. One, focus on your virtual options; one of the silver linings of the COVID pandemic is that so many more organizations and communities are meeting online. But, if like so many of us, you're all screened out by the end of the day or just don't dig Zoom, then see if you can find a community around some other activity or identity. Whether it's poker, ukulele, bowling, volunteering, or competitive crocheting, finding a crew that you can connect with on any level at all will make a difference.

Do *not not not* blame yourself. First arrows fly harder and faster when you're part of a minority or marginalized community. It's not always easy to remember that when you're neck deep in parenting chaos, which puts you at super high risk for second arrows. Support and connection are not optional, not indulgent. There's just no way to parent well without them.

How Connection Helps Our Kids

Here's the thing about kids: They're always watching us. Always. One the one hand, it sucks if you actually prefer to pee alone or if you're ever, you know, less than perfect. But on the other hand, all that watching means that they might actually maybe someday learn something from us about the power of connecting in moments of chaos and crisis.

Each time we respond to our toughest moments by remembering (ideally out loud) that sometimes life is really hard and every single one of us makes mistakes, our kids will learn how to develop that same perspective and not blame themselves for whatever went down. That's not to say they won't ever struggle with self-contempt—after all, they are only human—but at least they'll have a compassionate voice in their head when they do.

In addition, when our kids grow up in a community of trusted adults and we reach out to said trusted adults when things get rough, they benefit directly from the help and support of all those folks. Whether it's a friend who comes to jumpstart your car in the library parking lot or the one who picks up your kids from school when you're stuck in a meeting, showing our kids that they don't have to solve every problem on their own will make their entire lives easier and more manageable. In addition, they learn that connecting during times of stress and struggle isn't a sign of weakness; it's just what you do.

Finally, each time we come back to the present moment, our stress and anxiety will go down and we can be more patient and engaged with our children. And as our children are just beginning to develop their prefrontal cortexes (which is a nice way of saying that they literally don't have the brain cells to not freak out when they have to use the blue plate instead of the red one or their favorite pair of jeans isn't clean even though you asked them twelve times the day before if they had any dirty laundry to throw in the wash), they rely on our ability to stay calm and help them get calm when they can't.

Advanced Connection Practice: Talking to a Therapist

Lots of folks think talking to a therapist is like the worst version of going to the doctor. You wait until you can't tolerate your IBS or itchy rash or whatever mortifying thing is happening to your body and then you go into an uncomfortable room and put on a freaking paper dress and wait for a stranger to look you over with a critical eye before telling you exactly what's wrong with you. Then they write a prescription for the ridiculously expensive pill or ointment or procedure you'll need and tell you about all the ways it will screw up your sleep or make you gain fifteen pounds or obliterate the last remaining shred of your sex drive, all without even looking up from their clipboard or keyboard.

Thankfully, that's not even close to how therapy works, and if at any point in the process you feel like the therapist is just there to judge or diagnose you, then that's not the therapist for you. Therapy is about you and your therapist *working together* to help you improve your mental health, develop more skillful habits and coping skills, manage stressful situations, address relationship problems, and understand yourself better. Therapy is about finding a person you feel safe and comfortable with, someone you can talk to even when talking to someone feels like the last thing you want to do.

Now, you may be wondering if you even need to talk to a therapist. Maybe you've even googled something like "reasons to start therapy" and you came across lists of reasons ranging from insomnia and intrusive thoughts to problems with your relationships, eating habits, or emotions. Perhaps your depression, anxiety, panic, grief, or trauma history are making it hard to get through the day. Or maybe you're so overwhelmed that you're not even sure what the problem is or what would make it better, but you know something's not right. Whatever the reason, or even if you don't have a reason, you could probably benefit from therapy. I mean, who couldn't benefit from a safe space to talk about whatever's on your mind with a compassionate person?

Look, in a perfect world there would be a therapist on every block who charged nothing and also offered free coffee, and there would be childcare and time off work to go to therapy for every single one of us. But it's not a perfect world, and even if you can find a therapist with openings who takes your insurance, you may not have the money, support, and time to make it happen. Having said that, if you're having a hard time functioning in parenting, your relationships, your work, or just getting through your day, then therapy is almost certainly worth the hoops you might have to jump through in order to make it happen.

Choosing a Therapist

The process of finding a therapist can seem overwhelming, so let's break it down.

First, what can you afford? The rough reality is that if you can pay out of pocket without using insurance, you'll have a lot more options. But therapy sessions can cost eighty to two hundred dollars per hour, so most folks need to rely on their insurance. And if that's the case, your first step is to call your insurance company and figure out what your plan will cover.

> **Finding a therapist can be near impossible for many folks,** especially if you don't have insurance (and honestly, even if you do). This is fucked up and unfair and well, it just sucks. There's not a lot to be done about it other than a) remember that it's a systemic problem, not an individual one, and b) dig deep into the resources that are available to you, such as books (I've included some recommendations in the back of this book), apps, clergy, and the friends and family you trust.

Once you get clear on what you can afford and how you'll afford it, then the next step is to decide whether to meet in person or online. As both a therapist and therapee (not actually a word, but you know what I mean), I recommend in-person therapy whenever possible. Body language and other nonverbal communication provide important cues for therapists that can't always be communicated via screens, and I gotta tell you, there's nothing like leaving your house, going somewhere else, and leaving all your angst, anger, and anxiety in someone else's office before heading back to the chaos awaiting you at home.

If ideal isn't possible, then good is great. And virtual therapy is a very good alternative, especially if a) you can't find a therapist in your area, b) you don't have the time or childcare to get to an appointment across town each week, or c) you're stuck at home with a napping toddler. In addition, virtual therapy can also be more affordable than in-person options.

From there, there are a few other issues to consider:

- Would you prefer a male, female, or nonbinary therapist?
- Do you want someone who shares a specific trait or belongs to the same community as you? That's great if you can find it. But just to be clear, while it can helpful to work with someone who also identifies as queer or is Muslim or whatever it may be, a skilled therapist should be able to work effectively across communities and identities. And sometimes it can feel particularly freeing to work with someone who isn't a member of your tribe, as they might not bring any preconceived notions or judgment.
- Do you need someone who specializes in treating specific diagnoses or disorders? Most therapists can be quite helpful with depression, anxiety, and stress management, but if you're dealing with something more specific such as an eating disorder, alcohol or substance use, phobias, or bipolar disorder (for example), then you may benefit from finding a treater who has relevant experience and training.

- Do you have an opinion about the kind of work you want to do? Some therapists may focus on your childhood, relationship with your parents, and life history. However, if that doesn't sound like your cup of tea, other therapists will be skill-based, meaning they'll be more likely to focus on concrete strategies and practices to help address whatever you're struggling with. There are a lot of different ways for therapists to be helpful, and the truth is that many therapists use a mix of different approaches to help their clients. There isn't one style that's better than the others; what matters is that you find the right match for you.

In fact, finding someone who is a good match for you is the most important factor in determining the success of your therapy. This makes sense, right? It doesn't really matter how smart or experienced your therapist is or how many letters they have after their name if their tendency to uptalk sounds like fingernails on a chalkboard or the hour is filled with awkward silences or they never laugh at your jokes or they just don't seem to get you. What you want is someone who you feel safe and comfortable with and you feel like you can be honest and authentic with. It is completely and totally OK to speak with a few different therapists until you find the right match, and yes, this can take time, but it's absolutely worth it.

The Most Important Thing to Remember: Connection is the antidote to isolation, and it's the thing to do when you don't know what else to do.

CHAPTER SIX

Curiosity: The Life-Changing Magic of Exploring Your Experience

"I'm freaking out."

A good friend of mine said that to me during a recent walk. Her ten-year-old son, who we'll call Jack, was a hard-core bookworm and he had been begging for an eReader for several months. My friend hadn't wanted to get it for him for a bunch of different reasons. She and Jack both love paper books, and she didn't feel great about giving that up so he could spend even more time in front of a screen, even if it was to read a book. In addition, she was nervous about what he might end up reading; as she so accurately pointed out, there's just so much crap out there that he would have access to. But Jack was relentless so after a fair amount of research, she bought him a kid-friendly eReader for his birthday.

A week later, she was freaking out even more. "I set up the parental controls, we talked about the books he would be reading, and I thought I was on top of everything but then I got a notification that he downloaded a bunch of BDSM manga last night!"

I had no idea what BDSM manga was, but she explained that manga is a style of Japanese graphic novels and comic books, most of which are quite benign and appropriate for kids. BDSM, however, is a completely different story; it stands for bondage, discipline, sadism, and masochism. No judgment here, folks, but just not something my friend wanted her ten-year-old reading.

"I knew something like this would happen! I knew I shouldn't let Jack have an eReader, but it was the only thing he wanted and he just wouldn't let it go. The damn thing is marketed to kids, and I really thought I set it up right, but he managed to download that crap anyway. Is this what he's into? Is he already thinking about sex? The images in those books are creepy and violent and I am in wayyy over my head here. How did I screw this up? I am NOT equipped to handle this and I am freaking the fuck out."

I won't lie. My friend's experience totally triggered me and before I could even figure out what to say, my thoughts exploded. Now it was my turn to freak out about my daughters and sexual predators and unsafe sex and how the hell was I supposed to keep my girls safe in such a crazy world?? But I was working on this book and I was thinking about compassion, so I tried to calm myself down and think through my friend's situation and what I knew about her son. She was a thoughtful, careful mother and Jack was a reasonable kid. There had to be an explanation.

My friend had already decided to take away the eReader and was neck deep into wondering whether she should send Jack to therapy when I stopped her. "So, what does Jack have to say about this?"

Pause. Pause. "I haven't talked to him about it. But I am going to give him an earful."

I totally understood her impulse to lay the smack down, and I'd done it myself in the past. But I took a deep breath and suggested she start by just asking Jack what happened. I knew that my friend needed to get clear on what was actually going on with her son if she wanted to respond to him in the best way possible.

Curiosity Is the Antidote to Judgment

Judging the crap out of others, and ourselves, is one of the hallmark behaviors of Shitty Parent Syndrome. Hell, it's a hallmark behavior of being a human trying to make sense of chaos. Our brains don't like uncertainty and unpredictability, especially when the situation feels unsafe. When you don't know if that long squiggly thing on the ground is a stick or a snake poised to strike, jumping to conclusions might save your life. Judgment is an instinctive reaction, and it's also one that we have continued to practice so often and so frequently that we don't even realize we're doing it.

Here's a perfect example: Just this morning I went to make my beloved first cup of coffee, and when I went to push the button to start the brewing process, nothing happened. The blue light didn't come on. There was no magical *gurgle gurgle drip drip* sound.

I pushed it again.

Nothing.

Just silence and darkness. (And if this all sounds a bit dramatic to you, then clearly you don't have the same relationship to coffee as I do. It's OK. I forgive you.) I flipped out, and my thoughts exploded. My beloved coffee maker was broken. And I'm pretty sure my husband said something about this model—the perfect model—being discontinued. Not only would I not have my perfect cup of coffee this morning, I WOULD NEVER HAVE IT AGAIN.

I went into panic mode. My breathing got all shallow and my stomach twisted up and I lunged for my phone so I could look up how early my local Dunkin' Donuts opens and in the process I tripped over the cat, who made a horrible *marowr* sound before shooting me an awfully judgmental look and sprinting off. Fortunately, my husband came downstairs just at that moment and saw me frozen in the middle of the kitchen, clearly freaking out. I explained the situation—how our coffee maker was dead and we needed to get on eBay IMMEDIATELY and begin hoarding coffee makers. My husband ignored me as he calmly walked over to the machine, turned it around, looked at the back, and plugged it in.

And that right there is the difference between judgment and curiosity. I immediately jumped to the Worst Possible Outcome while my husband was able to get curious about what was going on with our coffee maker. (Although, for the record, I still think we should be buying backup coffee makers off eBay.)

On the off chance any of you read my coffee maker story as yet another example of a Hysterical Woman being saved by a Reasonable Curious Man, please don't. There are plenty of times in our marriage in which I, Reasonable Curious Wife, step in to assist my Freaking Out Husband. The only gender difference here is the one that age-old misogynistic BS stories have created out of thin air. Men judge the shit out of themselves and others just as often as women slow down and get curious. Judgment and curiosity are equal opportunity experiences.

The vast majority of us react to our own snafus by skipping straight past the trial and jury deliberation and heading straight to pulling out our gavels. BANG. Conversation over, decision made, conclusion reached. You screwed that up, and you are sentenced to a lifetime of believing you are a shitty parent. Each time we find ourselves guilty, we shut down any possibility for further exploration, clarity, or understanding, which is *exactly* what we need in that moment. How can we do things any differently in the future if we don't even understand what actually happened in the first place?

Each time we nail ourselves with a super judgy second arrow, we get so distracted by all the ways we suck that we don't have any brain space left to get curious about what actually happened, why it happened, how we feel about it, and what we might want to do next. And when we get all worked up and freaked out about whatever's going on, we're far more likely to default to a fight, flight, freeze, flip out, fix, or fawn response. And if we haven't taken the time to get clear on what's actually going on, our gut reaction isn't likely to be terribly effective.

We're told that curiosity is this beautiful and powerful perspective that we should nourish in our children, and it absolutely is. But curiosity can also be freaking terrifying, especially when we're pretty damn sure we don't want to know the answer to whatever it is we're supposed to be curious about. I'm not going to lie to you or pretend that curiosity will always feel good, because there will absolutely be times when exploring your own experience or the reason why your ten-year-old downloaded BDSM manga will uncover some fairly shitty first-arrow realities. But when you know that you won't have to face any second arrows, and you can trust that you'll treat yourself with compassion instead of contempt, curiosity doesn't seem nearly so scary.

The bottom line is that curiosity is the antidote to judgment, and it's awesome in a bunch of different ways:

- Curiosity brings us back to the present moment, which is the only place where we can get accurate information and insight (aka clarity) about what's actually going on.
- Curiosity has been linked to increased happiness and intelligence, stronger relationships, and a greater sense of meaning in life.
- Curiosity is a powerful and effective way to get out of our reactive reptile brains and bring our prefrontal cortexes online, which helps us calm down and think more clearly and creatively.
- Curiosity is an inherently kind response to whatever is going on. It's a way of communicating to ourselves and our children that we're not scared of or horrified by whatever we've done or are doing or aren't doing. No matter what, no matter how bad things may seem, we're worthy of time, attention, curiosity, and care.

Curiosity takes us a step beyond noticing. It's not just the ability to step back and realize what's happening; it's also about taking the time to get interested in our own experience, to wonder about it, and—wait for it—take our own responses seriously.

How Curiosity Helps

Curiosity doesn't just make us feel better, it actually makes our parenting lives easier and more manageable. Let's go back to little Jack and the BDSM manga. Once my friend was able to stop freaking out long enough to have a conversation with her son, she learned that he downloaded those books accidentally when he was looking for graphic novels. He had no idea what they were, he didn't like the pictures at all, and he wanted help getting them off his eReader.

Whew.

Crisis averted.

Of course, that conversation could have gone down a completely different road, and my friend could have found herself in the middle of an extremely awkward conversation about bondage with a ten-year-old boy. That would have sucked, for sure, and I wouldn't have blamed my friend for choosing to run from that faster than my daughter runs from a plate of spinach. But as much as we want to avoid the hard stuff in parenting, we all know that the sooner we can face the music, the sooner we can figure out exactly just how awful the current song is and exactly what it's going to take to turn down the volume or change the station altogether.

And then there's the Beach Day scenario—the one from Chapter 2 with the crappy air quality and asthmatic kid. At any point, from your first check of your weather app to the moment you lock yourself in the bathroom, you can notice what's happening and get curious about it. You can take a moment to notice that you've been wearing your shoulders like earrings all day, and wonder what's got you so tense. That might give you some insight into how anxious you are, which might help you realize that you've invested this one outing with a level of importance and power it probably doesn't merit. Even if you could go, it almost certainly wouldn't fix all of your doubts and worries about your daughter's functioning and your parenting. Or maybe if you were having a hard time getting curious yourself, you could call a friend who might ask you a few questions about what was going on and what you were worried about before thinking through solutions with you.

Even though all of this curiosity isn't going to fix the forecast or cure your daughter's asthma, it will shift your thinking from "This sucks and I'm a shitty parent" to "This sucks and sometimes parenting is rough, so where can I go from here?" It's possible you'll come up with a better plan than you might have otherwise, or you might end up with the same far-from-ideal outcome as you would have without your curiosity, but I guarantee, you'll feel way, way calmer and more confident at the end of the day.

And that's not nothing.

How to Be Curious

Most folks think of curiosity as asking questions. Who? What? When? Where? Why? What the hell were you thinking? And while questions can be an important part of a curiosity practice, let me be very clear: We're not going for an interrogation. This isn't about you shoving yourself into a crappy metal chair on the wrong side of a one-way mirror and blasting a spotlight in your face until you 'fess up to all your crimes. If any of your attempts at curiosity leave you feeling that way, that's a great time to turn to connection or kindness. (That's one of the cool things about self-compassion: There are a whole bunch of ways to practice it, and you get to choose what works for you in the moment.)

Curiosity also doesn't have to be a huge investigation into every feeling or experience you've ever had and all the ways in which your childhood screwed you up and led to this moment. I mean, I guess it could, if that's actually helpful, but it's not always necessary. And sometimes (as in the case of the not-so-broken coffee maker), all we need is a quick shift in perspective and a moment to look around.

Usually what we need is somewhere between a deep dive and a subtle shift in our thinking. In those moments, the goal is for curiosity to feel like that time when your beloved grandmother or favorite uncle sat down next to you on the couch, wrapped you in your favorite blanket, handed you a mug of hot cocoa, and asked, "So, what's going on?" And then they just listened. They didn't interrupt or raise an eyebrow or *tsk tsk* you even once. They just listened and occasionally asked a clarifying question and when you were done talking—like really done, not just pausing between sentences to take a breath—they asked a few more questions and considered your answers. And maybe they offered a few suggestions or ideas, but they were helpful suggestions or ideas that came from a place of deep understanding rather than snap judgments or freak-outs. Or maybe they didn't have any advice for you, but the fact that they weren't offended or horrified by anything you told them helped you feel less offended and horrified by your own experience. And just talking things through helped you get clear about what was actually going on and what you might do next.

If I had my way, we'd all have a kind uncle or fairy godmother waiting with a blanket and mug of something warm and yummy whenever we feel stressed or confused. But when that's not possible, we can create the same context for curiosity, which is an inherently kind approach to ourselves, our relationships, and our children.

One last note before you get started: It can be tempting to focus our curiosity on our kids or partners or whatever's happening around us, because honestly what the hell were they thinking and how exactly are we supposed to deal with the mess they left behind? But that's not curiosity; that's just our freak-out reaction looking for a place to land. Rather, our curiosity needs to start with ourselves and our own experience, and remember, we're going for loving grandma energy, not bad cop vibes.

Over the next several pages, you'll read a number of questions that may help you get curious. Remember: There aren't any right or wrong or good or bad answers, and you don't have to fix or solve anything. That's not what this is about. It's just about noticing, realizing, accepting, and understanding. This may not be so easy, especially if you're used to judging yourself, but you'll get there.

I'm going to offer a few steps for getting curious, but *please please please* remember that it's just about getting interested in what's going on for you and around you, and however you want to do that is totally cool.

Step 1: Notice. Noticing will help you get out of your reactive freak-out mode long enough so you can make an active, conscious choice about what to do next. The more freaked out you are, the more concrete and simple your noticing should be. Just notice anything in the present moment, anything from the color of your kitchen counter to the feeling of the fabric of your pants. If your mind keeps jumping back into fight, flight, freeze, flip out, fix, or fawn mode, then just keep noticing. Eventually you'll get calm and focused. (And if you're not freaking out, then head straight to Step 2.)

Step 2: Take your noticing even deeper. Here are a few questions that might help:

What are you doing? This might be seem like a really obvious question, but when we're in the midst of losing our minds, we often don't even realize that we're mindlessly scrolling through the same social media posts over and over again or biting our nails or snapping at our kids for merely glancing in our general direction.

What are you feeling? It might be immediately obvious that you're angry or anxious or confused or scared or exhausted. But identifying your emotions isn't always easy, so don't stress if you have no freaking idea what you're feeling. Your thoughts and bodily sensations might give you some important clues.

What are you thinking? Again, this isn't an angry-voice "What the hell were you thinking?" kind of question. This is more of a calm inquiry, a kind of "Hey there, buddy. What's going on in that noggin of yours?" It's just about directing your attention to the thoughts, ideas, memories, fantasies, worries, regrets, possibilities, or whatever else is bouncing around in your brain. You'll almost certainly get all caught up in those worries and regrets, which are likely to send you back into fight or flight mode. Nothing wrong with that, but as soon as you notice you're doing it, take a break and come back to curiosity.

What do you notice in your body? Are you grinding your teeth, tensing your jaw, or holding your shoulders up by your ears? Is your stomach in knots? Are you hungry? Thirsty? Do you have to pee? When was the last time you pooped? Is your chest feeling tight? Are you holding your breath? How's your head feeling? Do you have a headache? Are you feeling any soreness, stiffness, pain? What's going on with that tickle in the back of your throat or that hacking cough you've been ignoring? How's your back doing? And on a scale of "yawning occasionally" to "barely keeping your eyes open," just how exhausted are you?

If the thought of checking in with yourself is a bit too overwhelming or you're not sure where to start, the acronyms HALT and CALM can help get you started.

HALT. Whenever we feel **Hungry, Angry, Lonely, or Tired**, we're at high risk for spinning out, flipping out, and shitting all over ourselves. HALT is a good reminder to stop whatever you're doing for just a second and try to notice if you're:

Hungry, or have otherwise been ignoring or minimizing your basic needs (food, sleep, downtime, time with partners or friends, etc.),

Angry, or otherwise struggling with big, unpleasant feelings (anger, fear, sadness, confusion, overwhelm, grief, etc.),

Lonely, or feeling disconnected and/or unsupported, or

Tired. Wiped out, weary, exhausted. There are a ton of ways to be exhausted, including physical fatigue, mental fatigue (from thinking too hard for too long), emotional fatigue (from feeling too many intense feelings for too long), social fatigue (after being in stressful social situations), and soul exhaustion, when you've just been dealing with too much for too long and you have nothing left to give to anyone and you're not even sure what will make any of it better.

Each time you can HALT, and notice a) that you're suffering or struggling, and b) what you're struggling with, you're giving yourself a chance at compassion.

CALM. Take a moment to check in with your **Chest** (including your breathing), **Arms**, **Legs**, and **Mind**. You don't have to do any special relaxation techniques (although you can if you want to); it's just about checking in and getting curious. That should get you *calm* (Get it? See what I did there?) enough and give you the information you need to move on to Step 3.

Step 3: Ask yourself what you need. *And then take yourself seriously.* This is a deeply compassionate question that far too many of us parents rarely ask ourselves. Even if we do happen to realize that we could use a hot bath, a little help, or just five minutes of not a single person on the entire planet touching us or talking to us or coming anywhere near us, most of us race past those thoughts so quickly that we don't even a) notice them, or b) remember them, much less c) take them seriously.

Here are the questions I want you to ask yourself:

- What do I need right now to get through this moment?
- What do I need in general to make it through this day, this week, this month?

If you don't have the time or energy to think through this right now, can you make a little time for it? (And if your gut reaction is *NO, lady in the book, I really can't because I have a freaking job and three freaking kids and this freaking laundry isn't going to fold itself,* then well, I get that. I really do. But remember, the point of this whole book is to help you parent a little differently and a lot more compassionately, and taking your own needs seriously is a big part of that. So don't stress about the laundry and take a little time to get in touch with what you need.)

Now, it's entirely possible that even if you find the time to give this question some serious thought, you might not be able to figure out what you need. That's super common, and it doesn't mean you don't need anything or there's nothing that will make anything better. More likely, it just means you're exhausted and overwhelmed and you've been putting everyone else's needs ahead of your own for so damn long that you can't even begin to consider where you might fit in to all of this.

That's OK. You'll get there. And in the meanwhile, there are a few different ways to figure out what you need.

Find out what's been helpful for other folks. This is a great way to start connecting or deepen a connection with a friend or fellow parent. Talk about what's going on for you and ask them what's been helpful to them. How are they coping? And even if their response is "I have no freaking clue and nothing's going to help," then at least you'll know you're not alone while you keep figuring this out.

Experiment a little bit. Even if you're not sure *exactly* what you need, try a few things. Unless what you actually need is a colonoscopy (in which case, sorry about that!), then you've got a bunch of options for taking care of yourself and treating yourself with compassion. This isn't rocket science; it's often just about getting more sleep, or setting up a couple of carpools so you don't have to spend every afternoon schlepping around town, or making a point to eat breakfast every morning, or taking yourself for a walk outside instead of answering emails during your lunch hour, or bowing out of a kindergarten soccer game so you can grab coffee with a friend instead. Try to notice how you're feeling during and after each of these activities. Did it help? Do you feel more connected and less stressed? If so, that might give you a sense that what you need is more sleep or less driving or more time with friends, and you can make a plan to build that into your life more often. And even if what you really need is far more significant than a walk at lunch, these small steps can go a long way toward helping you get the clarity you need to identify the bigger issues.

Ask for help. If you can't give yourself what you need, can anyone else? Can you reach out to a friend or family member or neighbor or therapist and ask for what you need? And if this feels really hard or just not your thing, remember that when you get the help you need, you'll be a better parent and you'll be modeling an important life skill for your kids. Oh, and you'll be giving your friends and family members permission to ask for help when they need it, which is pretty awesome too.

Step 4: Get curious about the content you're struggling with *and* the context you're living in. First, the *content*—the actual worry that's keeping you up at night. What's distracting you when you're trying to focus? What's that thorn in your side? A conflict with a family member? Burnout at work? Anxiety about your kid's recent test results? A freaking toothache that you can't seem to ignore away? Stress about an upcoming holiday? That estimate from the mechanic that you really can't afford? The horrifying news headlines that won't stop coming? The latest racist incident in your community?

We've all got something, and most of us have more than one thing most of the time. And most of the time we react to whatever's going on with whatever version of fight, flight, freeze, flip out, fix, or fawn we tend to practice the most. Sometimes those reactions work out well enough, but more often than not, all that judgment and shame a) doesn't solve the problem, and b) triggers the crap out of our Shitty Parent Syndrome.

But when we can get curious about whatever we're struggling with and why we're struggling with it, we'll get calmer and clearer about whatever's going on, which will help us think creatively and confidently about what to do next. Here's the thing, though: You're not going to want to do this, because thinking about this stuff without immediately leaping into action is going to feel bad. It's going to feel uncomfortable or scary or confusing or sad. And most of us don't like feeling any of those things, which is why we tend to reach for our phones or jump up to unload the dishwasher or grab a glass of wine or do whatever it is we do when we don't want to do the thing we have to do.

But when you can sit with your situation long enough to get curious, you might actually get some answers. Let's think about how this might play out on a Beach Day. Instead of snapping at everyone who crosses your path or blaming yourself for not being able to control the weather or comparing yourself to all those other Beachy-Ass Parents, just sit down for a second, take a few deep breaths, consider the following questions, and *please please please* if you do nothing else in this chapter, *listen to the answers and take them seriously. Do not blow yourself off, and try not to judge yourself for whatever you notice or realize.*

- What am I thinking, feeling, and/or doing? What's going on in my body?
- Who or what am I worried about / scared of / angry at / having other big feelings about?

- Who or what am I *really* worried about? (Sometimes you have to dig pretty deep to get to the bottom of this one.)
- What can I control? What can't I control?
- What can I do about the situation today?
- Do I need help? If so, who could help me? How can I reach out to them for help?
- What's the story I want to tell about this situation someday?
- What advice would my beloved grandmother or favorite uncle or best friend give me right now?
- What is the most skillful choice I could make right now?

In all likelihood, you might not like the answers you come up with. That's OK. This is a judgment-free zone. Or at least a notice-your-judgment-and-then-try-to-let-it-go-because-you're-only-human zone. You can handle it. And no matter what it is, it will pass. It might pass like a damn kidney stone, but it will pass. And again, you might arrive at the same shitty outcome, but you won't have used your crap map to get there, and you won't have been hit by a single second arrow along the way.

If getting curious about the content of what you're dealing with is too stressful or leaves you feeling too overwhelmed, or if it's triggering your Shitty Parent thoughts, then maybe it's time to consider the *context* of your situation. Remembering the bigger picture will help you have more compassion for yourself and your situation.

> **We parents tend to blame ourselves for child-related challenges** and struggles that have very little to do with us and a whole lot to do with a lack of information, support, and resources. It doesn't matter how much you care or how hard you're working: it's nearly impossible to feel like a good parent when you have to choose between paying the rent and covering the co-pay on your child's latest ER visit. But when we're exhausted and overwhelmed, it can be damn hard to figure out what we can control and change and when we need to remember to let ourselves off the hook. If you find yourself struggling with this issue, check in with the wise folks in your community—friends, doctors, therapists, elders, or anyone else whose advice you trust. They might have a clearer perspective on the situation than you do.

Here are a few questions you might want to consider:

- What else is going on in my life right now?
- What other stressors am I dealing with in my personal or professional life?
- What else am I worried about / scared of / angry at / having other big feelings about?
- Am I dealing with any big changes, transitions, or crises right now? What about my close friends, kids, and family?
- What time of year is it? Am I starting or in the middle of a particularly challenging month or season?

- Are there any significant holidays coming up? Any major anniversaries, including anniversaries of painful losses or divorces? (And bear in mind that even positive, joyful holidays and anniversaries can be a source of stress.)

- Have I been eating, drinking, sleeping, shopping, gambling, [insert your favorite coping mechanism / vice here], more than usual lately? (The answer to this question may give you useful clues as to how you're *actually* doing.)

- How's my health and the health of the people and/or animals I care about?

- How exhausted am I? How have I been sleeping at night?

Remember, the goal of asking all of these questions—and listening to your answers—is to get a little perspective on everything you're dealing with and cut yourself a whole lotta slack. If you start to feel overwhelmed by what you realize, that's probably because you're in an overwhelming situation. Once again, nothing to judge or blame yourself for, just another opportunity for you to practice. And just to be abundantly clear, practice does not make perfect, but it does make it a whole lot easier (but nobody ever says that because "practice makes easier" isn't nearly as catchy or alliterative).

Before we get to Step 5, I want you to know that Steps 2, 3, and 4 on this list (deeper noticing and getting curious about your needs, content, and context) can really happen in any order, depending on what comes naturally to you and makes the most sense for whatever you're dealing with and how you tend to think about your situation. The first time you try this whole curiosity thing, it's going to feel all weird and awkward and cheesy and you're gonna want to blow it off and hop on over to Instagram instead because you just discovered a new account devoted entirely to honey badgers and you're pretty damn sure you've found your daughter's kindred spirit. Please don't do that. Stick with your curiosity, and, whenever possible, take the time you need for yourself before you move on to your kids.

Step 5: Get curious about your kids. OK, I know what you're thinking. You're thinking that this is what you really need to be curious about because if you can just figure out what's wrong with your kid and how to solve their problems or make them happy, then that's all you need to do because that's what good parents do and then you'll be a good parent, which is all you freaking wanted in the first place. And that's all fine and dandy, except for the part where sometimes we can't figure out what's wrong with our kid and their problems aren't freaking solvable and even if they are, you're not going to make them happy, at least not in any ongoing way, because that's just not how life works.

That's the first reason I put your kids at the bottom of this curiosity list. The second reason is because it's pretty unlikely that you'll be able to deal effectively and empathically with whatever you figure out about your kids if you're a giant ball of stress and shame. So put on your freaking oxygen mask and fill your cup or whatever metaphor works for you; the point is that the calmer and clearer you are with regard to the current situation, the less likely you'll be to react impulsively or unhelpfully.

So take a few minutes to chill out and get curious about what you're dealing with (unless you're dealing with a screaming toddler or door-slamming tween, in which case you'll do the best you can to get the situation under control and you will absolutely positively 100 percent not get all pissy or shamey at yourself for however you handled it), and then—and only then—you'll move on to your kiddo. We'll dig into this more deeply in Chapter 8, How to Compassion the Crap Out of Your Kids.

Again, you might not like the answers you find. More often than not, the hardest parenting moments, the ones that send us into a complete tizzy, aren't fixable—for us or our kids. I mean, if they were fixable, you probably would have fixed them by now, right? Or they're potentially fixable, but the fix takes a crapload of time and money and energy and appointments with specialists who are totally booked up for the next six months and only have openings in the middle of the workday and fuuuuuuuuuck. Either way, or if you happen to be in a crappy headspace or unshakably grumpy and all this curiosity stuff lands you back in JudgyTown, well, do your best to just notice that judgment without getting sucked into it. And if you can't do that, because, well, let's be honest, that's damn hard to do sometimes, that's when you go back to connection and kindness.

How Curiosity Helps Our Kids

When our daughters were still in preschool, my husband and I took them to the local street fair. They were having a great time playing on the inflatables, listening to the live bands, and begging us for five dollars so they could throw a ball at a tower of bottles and win a fifty-cent toy. Just as I was about to shell out even more cash so they could fish for plastic ducks, one of the girls started whining. Her whining soon escalated to a full-on, limp-bodied meltdown, right there in the middle of the street, in full view of all of our neighbors and friends.

What the hell? We had literally given this kid everything she asked for all day, and this was how she responds? I mean, she was little, so it's not like I was expecting a formal thank-you or anything, but she could have at least kept it together until we got home. What kind of spoiled, ungrateful kid was I raising? I got all cranky and resentful and started snapping at her, which didn't help anything.

Flash forward five minutes to me grabbing my daughter's hand and pulling her down the street. "That's it. We're going home!" My daughter was crying. I was fuming. We were halfway home when we passed a neighborhood restaurant and suddenly it hit me.

She was hungry.

My daughter had inherited some seriously strong hangry genes from me and tended to tank quickly if we missed a snack or were late to a meal. She wasn't trying to be disrespectful or ungrateful; she was just doing what four-year-olds do when they get so distracted by bouncy houses and free Frisbees that they forget to eat and their parents forget to feed them. Nine years later, she's finally old enough to notice when she's hungry and get herself a snack, but back then the job was on me.

If I had taken the time to get curious about what was going on with my kiddo instead of jumping to conclusions and judging her for being a spoiled little brat and judging myself for being the kind of parent who raises spoiled brats, I might have realized that she just needed a snack. That's all.

Our curiosity practice benefits our children directly each time it helps us get information and insight about what's actually going on with our kids so we can respond to them from a place of calm clarity rather than freaking out all over them. In that moment, I was able to get my daughter a snack, help her calm down, apologize for snapping at her, and talk to her about how to notice when she's hungry. Best of all, perhaps, I was able to let go of my simmering anxiety about raising an entitled little jerk of a kid (which, for the record, she's totally not).

And when we can notice what's going on with our children and make the connections they can't yet make, we're teaching them to do the same. If we were to react to every difficult or confusing parenting moment by freaking out, that's what our kids will learn how to do. But when we can slow down and get curious about what might be going on for ourselves and our kiddos, we're teaching them how to do that instead. We're showing our children, in the most powerful way possible, that there's another way to handle hard moments. We can put down our second arrows and turn to compassion instead.

Advanced Curiosity Practice: Journaling

Sometimes it's just too hard to think. Or we haven't quite figured out how to think about our thoughts. Or our brains are too damn addled and we can't get enough space from our thoughts to actually be curious about them. Or we can't remember what we realized long enough to let it really sink in. Or perhaps no matter how hard we try, we can't quite figure out how to be curious in a way that doesn't feel like we're interrogating ourselves.

Whatever the reason, putting pen to paper can be a super effective way to get out of your own mind and into your own experience. Even if you think you're not a writer, don't stress. Nobody gives two shits if your sentence structure sucks or you still have no idea how to spell "irritating," as in "irritating AF," because nobody's ever going to read it. Your journaling isn't about writing something good or getting to the right answers; it's just about getting a little more information and insight about what's going on without getting all twisted up in your own thoughts and judgments.

A few things that might help you get started on a journaling practice:

- You don't have to write every day. You really don't. You can write whenever you want or whenever you need to. It's true that the more you practice something, the easier it gets, but the more you focus on being perfect or not breaking the streak, the harder it's going to be to pick up your pen again when you really need to.

- Despite what I keep saying about pens, you don't have to actually use a pen. You can absolutely use your computer or tablet. You can use a random piece of paper or a fancy journal or a pencil or a crayon or a Sharpie or a fork dipped in ink. Whatever works for you is perfect.

- Some folks prefer to just start with a blank page and write whatever comes to mind, while an empty page or screen is absolutely horrifying to others. If the thought of starting from scratch makes you want to stick that pencil right in your eye, then it's OK to give yourself a little structure. Write out some of the questions from this chapter, or any other questions that work for you, and then answer those. And, if the thought of answering questions conjures up horrible memories of elementary school worksheets, then scale it back and pick a couple of words that might get you going, such as "thoughts," "feelings," or "CALM."

- If the words just aren't coming, you can always start with drawing or doodling. Either of those will help you get calm and focused enough to find your words.

- You can go back and read what you wrote, or not.

- You can keep what you wrote, or you can delete or shred it as soon as you're done.

The Most Important Thing to Remember: Curiosity is the opposite of judgment, and it's the most effective way to calm down and get some clarity when you're overwhelmed or confused.

CHAPTER SEVEN

Kindness: You're Not a Monster. Parenting Is Hard.

I recently asked a group of parents about the kindest thing anyone ever did for them. Not surprisingly, a lot of the responses were about friends who brought over meals, cleaned houses, or took care of the kids during a crisis. I can certainly relate; my twenty-month-old daughter fractured her leg the day before I was due to give birth to my second daughter. By the time we got home from a long day at the hospital, a friend had dropped off toys our toddler could play with on the couch and my sister had arranged for a local deli to deliver a week's worth of meals. Not only were the toys and food incredibly helpful, but I felt supported rather than judged.

However, of all the kindness stories I've heard recently, this one from my friend Amy really caught my attention:

> *My firstborn was horribly colicky as a baby. Unless I was moving or nursing him, he was wailing. I was dealing with postpartum depression and was really a mess. I was at a new moms' group meeting and talked a little bit about how impossible it was to get the baby to sleep. Another mom of a slightly older infant told me she had been there and knew how hard it was. She wrote her phone number on a piece of paper and told me I could call her anytime (she emphasized that . . . anytime, even in the middle of the night) if I needed support. Somehow I knew she meant it. I kept her number on*

the fridge for months. I never called her but somehow knowing I could call got me through some really rough times.

At first glance, this story doesn't make any sense at all. I mean, some random woman—who we'll call Compassionate Courtney—gives Amy her phone number, which then gathers dust on the fridge. And this becomes an act of kindness that Amy remembers for years, even though she never freaking called the number?? I mean, COME ON. Courtney didn't actually do anything other than hand over her phone number, which she almost certainly knew Amy wouldn't use.

And now she gets to be the heroine of Amy's story?

That's bonkerballs.

Except it's not really.

What Courtney did was such a powerful example of the kindness of compassion that not only did I nickname her Compassionate Courtney but we're also going to devote several paragraphs to exploring just how awesome her response was.

1. First, and perhaps most importantly, **Courtney noticed that Amy was struggling, she took it seriously, and she responded with kindness.** There are lots of different reasons to be kind, including a) doing something nice for someone because they did something kind for you and you feel compelled to return the favor, b) because your kids are watching you and you feel compelled to be a good role model, c) you just came out of church or synagogue or mosque and you're feeling the kindness vibes big time, d) you saw a bumper sticker about performing random acts of kindness and senseless beauty and you happen to be in a good

mood and the sun is shining so you give the guy at the taco stand an extra big tip, or e) you were just a huge dick to someone and your guilt is driving you to try and make things right.

Don't get me wrong, those forms of kindness—actually, any forms of kindness—are great. Huge fan over here. But they're not the same as choosing to be kind in response to suffering. Kindness may seem like a pretty obvious choice in tough times, but it's not always that easy. It's human nature to want to turn away from suffering, to ignore it, minimize it, or try to fix it or offer advice on how to deal with it. And while some of the fixing and advice-giving might be helpful at times (more on that later), it's not the same as showing up and sticking around even when things are rough or unpleasant or downright horrifying, and responding in a friendly, generous, and considerate way. Which is exactly what Courtney did.

2. **Courtney's response wasn't just kind, it was respectful.** Kindness is the opposite of contempt, which is the feeling or belief that someone or something isn't worthy of our respect or approval. Courtney also had a colicky baby, and I have to imagine that she didn't feel like she had a ton of free time or extra energy, and I'd bet my right arm that she wasn't looking for someone else to wake her up in the middle of the night—especially that lady with the wild eyes she just met at the support group. Courtney could have suggested that Amy call the local parenting hotline or talk to her pediatrician, but she didn't do that. She gave Amy her phone number, and she did it in such a way that Amy knew her offer was serious. I can't think of a clearer or more powerful way to communicate respect. That paper may have only had ten digits

on it, but what it said was "Your struggles are real, and they matter. You're not alone. You matter and you're worth my time and energy, so call me anytime."

3. Courtney didn't try to fix anything, which is actually one of the kindest things we can do in response to suffering. She didn't give Amy a list of books to read or suggest some super-secret strategy for fixing colic (because PS THAT DOESN'T EXIST). When we offer advice or suggestions in moments of pain or confusion, the underlying message—whether we actually mean it or not—is that the person should have done something differently. They should have done something better. If they're having a hard time, it's because they didn't work hard enough or try hard enough or they're just not good enough. And whether or not that's true, that's a pretty sharp arrow to hurl at someone when they're already down.

Nobody likes unsolicited advice. As well intentioned as it may be, unsolicited advice almost always feels like someone else is trying to fix us, and that never feels good. It can be damn hard not to offer a solution when we have one, but the reality is that unless someone explicitly asks for your advice, they probably don't want it or aren't in a headspace to hear it—*even when it might actually be helpful.*

4. Courtney didn't offer more than she had. She didn't invite Amy back to her house, she didn't offer to take Amy's baby for her, she didn't hand over her address with an invitation to stop by any time. Courtney didn't throw herself under the bus in order to help Amy. She did what she could with what she had.

5. By sharing her phone number instead of advice, **Courtney tapped into the power of both connection and curiosity.** Not only did she tell Amy that she wasn't alone, and that she (Courtney) had struggled the same way, but she opened up the possibility for further connection. In addition, asking someone to call you up to talk is pretty much the definition of being curious. (Unless, of course, you launch into some crazy long monologue about your own shit or immediately start outlining all the ways in which the other person sucks or everything they should be doing differently or better. That's definitely not being curious, so please don't do that.)

6. **Courtney didn't reach out because she was trying to make herself or Amy feel better.** She did it because Amy was in pain. This is a nuanced and very specific point, but it's a crucially important one. Feeling better is a common side effect of compassion, but it isn't the goal. It can't be the goal because we can't control our feelings, and basing your success on something you have no control over is an epically bad idea. Once we get hung up on feeling better, then we assume it's not OK to feel bad. And then we start judging and blaming ourselves for that. *Thwack thwack thwackity thwack.*

So, Courtney's awesome and what she did was awesome. But please don't misunderstand me; I'm not suggesting you start handing out your phone number to every struggling person you come across. That's not gonna end well. I'm just hoping you can get clarity about what kindness is and what it isn't, so you can throw a little bit back at yourself whenever possible. Just to review, the kindness of self-compassion is about:

- Noticing your suffering and taking it seriously.
- Treating yourself with respect rather than contempt.
- Setting aside the need to fix yourself or solve the problem. I'm not saying you won't ever get to the fixing part, but when you start from a place of kindness, you'll bring a lot more clarity, creativity, and confidence to the situation.
- You don't need to go over the top with your kindness. Just do what you can with what you have.
- Connection and curiosity are inherently kind, so they're a great place to start, especially if you're not sure what else to do.
- Remember, you're not treating yourself with kindness because you need to feel better. You're doing it because you feel bad. And that's enough.

How to Treat Yourself with Kindness: The Arrows of Kind Self-Care

So, you've just been hit by a first arrow of life. Whether it's a colicky baby or a teen who needs braces and holy hell those things are expensive or a weird lump that you really should get checked out or a fellow mom who just told you that there was pot at the party both of your kids went to last weekend, the shit just hit the fan. Now, imagine if instead of getting shot by a second arrow, a fluffy arrow of kindness carrying a basket holding your dad's homemade doughnuts and a perfect cup of coffee and your favorite magazine or newspaper and maybe even a housekeeper, a babysitter, a copy of this book, and Courtney's phone number landed on your doorstep.

Sadly, that particular second arrow doesn't actually exist, but a bunch of other ones do. And no matter how painful, overwhelming, or confusing our experience is, no matter how far astray we've gone, and no matter how exhausted and stressed we are, we can always, always respond with kindness. We can always choose to pull a different arrow—an arrow of kind self-care—out of our quiver.

Now before we jump into the juicy details of kind self-care, let me remind you that **self-care is not self-improvement**. This is really freaking important, and if you're like most folks I know, it's going to take awhile for this idea to really take hold in your wary brain. In the meanwhile, engrave it on your favorite bracelet or tattoo it on your forehead (backward, of course) or whatever it takes for you to remember that the point of self-care is NOT to make yourself feel better or get in better shape or get your shit together. I'm not saying self-improvement is a bad thing; it's just a different thing, and when we confuse the two, then everything becomes about trying to improve ourselves, which means we don't get a single moment of our day when we aren't reminded of how we could be doing better. And that is FUCKING EXHAUSTING.

Over the rest of this chapter, we're going to explore ten kind self-care strategies that you can practice regularly. The first four practices—kind self-talk, kind stories, singletasking, and setting boundaries—can become regular injections of kindness that will help top off your tank and make you more resilient in the face of all the first arrows of life. The next six practices—sip, snack, stretch and soak, snuggle, song or show, and sleep—are great any time, but they're also especially powerful alternatives to those shitty second arrows.

The First Four Arrows of Kind Self-Care: Self-Talk, Stories, Singletasking, and Setting Boundaries

Kind Self-Talk

A friend recently texted me about her son, one of my daughter's fifth-grade classmates. Apparently, like my daughter, her son was shoving all his math worksheets into the bottom of his backpack rather than putting them in his math folder. She sent me a picture of the crumpled, torn pages along with a string of messages, ending with "Ugh. I'm such a shitty parent."

I think we can all agree that a fifth grader's inability to properly file his math papers has nothing to do with my friend's parenting skills. And I actually think my friend would agree with that assessment; that's not the issue here. The issue here is how quickly that final text came through. It's not like my friend thought about her son shoving his papers into his backpack and came to the carefully considered conclusion that it clearly meant she was a shitty parent. Nope. Those five words flowed off her fingertips faster than her own name.

She'd been thinking them a lot.

My guess is that she hadn't even realized how often she'd been thinking of herself as a shitty parent, but make no mistake about it: That crappy self-talk was absolutely impacting my friend's mood and her confidence in her ability to parent well. In addition, it left zero headspace for her to a) get clear on why her son kept crumpling his papers and why she cared so much, and b) think creatively about how to either fix it or get over it.

Once we start paying attention to our own thoughts—without getting sucked into them—one of the first things most of us notice is how poorly we talk to ourselves. We say things to ourselves that we wouldn't say to our worst enemy, or at least not to their faces:

- I'm a shitty parent.
- I'm screwing up my kids.
- I totally blew that one.
- Other parents are happier, fitter, calmer, more organized, more patient, more blah blah blah whatever than I am.

We're not just saying those things to our faces; we're repeating them over and over again, drilling them into our consciousness. And most of us have no idea we're even doing it.

So, that sucks.

Fortunately, kind self-talk is a super simple strategy that makes life feel so much easier to handle. Once you learn how to evict that gremlin who's taken up residence in your brain, you can make space for a cheerleader or best friend or just a cheerful little puppy who follows you around (in a not-at-all-annoying way, of course) and loves you no matter what. Fortunately, you don't actually have to get a puppy in order to change the voice in your head. Here's what to do instead:

Keep on noticing. Not to keep beating that deader-than-dead horse, but this is actually a super important (if dead) horse. If you don't notice each time you criticize, abuse, harass, demean, doubt, or undermine yourself, then you can't change it.

Don't beat yourself up or feel ashamed or guilty for whatever you notice. Try not to dig into those thoughts or fight with them or give them any more time than you already have. Just because you've been thinking things for a long time doesn't mean they're true. Seriously. You can think you're capable of teleportation every minute of every day of your life but you still gotta get in the car and drive your butt across town for your kid's recital. So regardless of how intense or frequent your shitty self-thoughts are, just keep on noticing them and letting them go. It's going to take time, but it will get better.

Try talking to yourself in a kind way—whatever that looks and sounds like for you. Remind yourself of your common humanity, get curious about your situation, and focus on understanding, acceptance, and forgiveness. This may sound incredibly cheesy, but it doesn't have to be that way. Instead of coming at yourself with vague platitudes, try using your own words, the words you might use when comforting a good friend.

Learning to speak to yourself with kindness is like learning to speak a new language. It can be incredibly hard to find the words, and they might feel strange rolling off your tongue. That's OK. It doesn't mean you're doing anything wrong. It just means you're doing something new, and it will get easier. Here are a few tricks that might help:

- One of the quickest and most effective ways to learn a new language is to spend time with native speakers. Reach out to friends who will speak the language of compassion to you. Call them, text them, do whatever it takes. And if you're not sure how to start the conversation, go back to Chapter 5 and the conversation with Happy Muffin Mom on your front porch. Consider your options for opening up about whatever you're struggling with, choose the one that seems easiest, and start there. And when your friends respond with compassion, *listen to them*. You can't learn a new language if you don't freaking listen to how it's spoken.

- If you can't find your own words, use someone else's. In the heat of the moment, a quote, mantra, prayer, or the lyrics from a favorite song can be incredibly helpful. If you have a little more time on your hands, turn on your favorite podcast or pick up your favorite book. It doesn't have to be self-help; anything that calms you down, helps you get a break from your shitty self-talk, and leaves you feeling more connected and/or curious is a great choice.

- Keep practicing. It will get easier. Here are a bunch of examples you can use, or you can come up with your own. Write them on sticky notes and wallpaper your house and car and baby stroller in them.
  - It's a hard day. It's a hard moment. That's OK.
  - I'm a good mother / father / parent.
  - This sucks, but it will pass.
  - I love and accept myself just as I am.
  - I can take the time to take care of myself.
  - That lady in the book says I'm not a shitty parent so maybe I'll believe her.
  - Parenting is really fucking hard. That doesn't mean I'm doing it wrong.
  - I'm not alone. This is hard for all of us.
  - Just breathe. Keep breathing.
  - What am I thinking or feeling? What do I need right now?

Kind self-talk is one of your most important self-compassion strategies. If, for some weird reason that actually doesn't exist, you can focus only on one form of self-care, this is the one. You can practice it anywhere, at any time, and once you start noticing your shitty self-talk and treating yourself with kindness instead, it will be like you put down a giant weight you didn't even realize you were carrying.

Tell Yourself a Kind Story

Let's go back to my friend and her son with the eReader and BDSM manga. That's a story she's going to be telling for a long time, and there are about a million different ways she could frame it:

A) "It's the freaking eReader industrial complex out to screw innocent parents across the globe."

B) "My son is a closet sex maniac. I'm doomed."

C) "THIS—this right here—is why children shouldn't read graphic novels."

D) "I am the worst parent ever in the history of the whole entire universe."

E) "I'm just trying to remember that I'm part of the first generation of parents to ever give their kids eReaders because these things literally didn't exist until a few years ago. But kids have been reading inappropriate stuff since the printing press was created, so if it wasn't this device, it probably would have been something else. We're all just doing the best we can, and I'll get through this one."

Now, I know that I've gone on and on in this book about how there's no such thing as right and wrong or good and bad but seeing as how I'm the one writing this book, I get to completely contradict myself and tell you that in this particular case there is ABSOLUTELY A RIGHT ANSWER.

And in case it's not abundantly clear, that answer is E. (OK, and maybe a little bit A, but really E.)

Finding your way to a compassionate, connected, kind story is related to self-talk, but it's about crafting a new narrative, a new story about what's happening—both in the moment when the shit hits the fan, and in our lives overall. It's about making sense of the big picture and of who we are in the world in the kindest, most compassionate way possible.

Singletask (Or at Least, Lesstask)

Singletasking is the opposite of multitasking. It's about choosing to do just one thing at a time and doing our best to keep our attention focused on whatever it is we're doing. That's the goal whenever possible, and when it's not, the goal is lesstasking (a word I absolutely just made up, in case you were wondering), which is about setting aside as much as you can—at least for the moment.

At this point, you're probably thinking I'm completely insane because if you were to suddenly stop doing a bajillion things at once, the laundry would never get folded and dinner would never get made and your work emails would go unanswered and your kids would have to figure out their bananapants math homework on their own.

Oh, and you're probably wondering what the hell does this have to do with kindness?

Great question. I'm so glad you asked it.

Imagine that your best friend just texted you. She's a mess and needs your help. You drop off your kids at school, reschedule a meeting, and head over. When you get to your friend's house, she's sitting at the kitchen table, looking defeated, overwhelmed, and completely stressed-out. Her tears and words start flowing at the same time as she tells you about the results of her kid's psych testing and all the specialists she's supposed to call and appointments she's supposed to make and how she just doesn't have time for this right now because she's totally behind on a major work thing and she still hasn't dealt with the shitshow from last weekend's basement flood and her house is a freaking mess and she's pretty sure the cat needs to have some teeth extracted and the dishwasher is definitely on its last legs.

Let's think about how you would respond.

I'm pretty certain you wouldn't take that opportunity to point out the unfolded laundry on the dining room table or the dishes in the sink. And I know you wouldn't pull out your phone and show your friend the latest shitty headlines or social media updates or bring up her jerk of an ex and how he should be helping more. You definitely wouldn't go off about how if she thinks dealing with specialists is rough now just wait until her kid gets to middle school because that's when the shit really hits the fan.

The point is, you wouldn't. You wouldn't do any of that because a) you're not a dick, which means that, b) even if you are absolutely convinced that your own life would fall apart without multitasking, you would never shoot those same second arrows at someone you care about. Instead, you find a box of tissues, make her a cup of coffee, and maybe even grab a pen and paper and help wade through the weeds she's stuck in until she can get a little clarity. Eventually, you come up with a plan. First things first, one thing at a time, she'll get through it.

This may sound a lot like planning, and sometimes a little planning is required in order to singletask. And sometimes it's not. Whatever it takes, it's worth it because multitasking is just a bunch of second-arrow bullshit. It stresses us out, makes life feel harder, and leaves us feeling less competent and capable. When we focus on doing just one thing at a time, we're calmer, less likely to screw up, and more likely to notice whatever it is that needs noticing. Singletasking and lesstasking are inherently kind responses to whatever is going on; choosing to set down some of the flaming swords we're juggling decreases our stress and makes it far less likely that we'll drop, forget, break, or lose something (including our own minds) in the process. And it just makes everything feel soooo much easier.

In an ideal world, we'd all have a friend or fairy godmother who could drop by each time we're overwhelmed and help us get focused. Sadly, that doesn't exist, because if it did, the aforementioned fairy godmother wouldn't just help us get focused; she'd actually fix all the damn problems so we could chill on the couch with that movie we've been wanting to watch but is too inappropriate for the kids, who we currently don't have to worry about because they're with their fairy godmother. Whatever. You get the point. The other point, of course, is that we can do this for ourselves. We can extend ourselves the kindness of choosing to singletask (or lesstask) at any time. We can remind ourselves that we don't have to fix or handle or take care of or deal with everything right now in this moment. It's just about noticing when we're trying to do too many things at once and choosing to put down our phones or close our laptops or let go of the triggering memories or unhelpful worries so we can take just one minute to actually listen to our child's nagging question about why potties are actually called toilets.

If the mere thought of doing just one thing at a time is making you break out in hives, remember, we're not going for perfect. If you like to watch TV while you fold laundry or go for walks while you talk with your friends or listen to music while you cook dinner, then rock on. But when you're dealing with a complicated or stressful situation, or emotions are running high, or your kids need attention, well, those are perfect opportunities to set down as many of those flaming swords as you can and treat yourself with kindness.

Set Boundaries

Lots of folks (and to be honest, folks, mostly women) have a hard time setting and holding our boundaries. We say yes when we want to say no, we agree to carpools and committees and activities and events we have zero interest in or time and energy for, and we make promises to our children that make us cringe every time we think about them.

We do this because we think we should; it's what good parents do, right? Or maybe we think we have something to atone for. Or maybe we're worried about what other people will think or we don't want to make them feel bad. But shaming or guilting ourselves into doing something—anything—we don't want to do is pretty much the opposite of kindness. If you're having a hard time wrapping your mind around this, think about a friend or family member or fellow parent or anyone you care about. How would you advise them? We both know you would pull a Nancy Reagan and tell them to Just Say No.

And that's exactly what I want you to do for yourself. Just say no.

Or no thank you.

Or not now.

Or not ever.

Setting and holding your boundaries might not feel good in the moment, but that's OK. Remember, kindness isn't about making yourself feel better, and it's definitely not about prioritizing anyone else's feelings over your own.

The Next Six Practices: Sip, Snack, Stretch or Soak, Snuggle, Song or Show, Sleep

As you read through this list, the first thing you might notice is that this all seems like really basic self-care, and it is. But as I hope you've realized by now, giving yourself even the most basic self-care is a powerful form of compassion, and compassion makes life and parenting so much easier and better and more sparkly, which is to say that this stuff is super basic but also super awesome so you should take it seriously but not too seriously because that might stress you out, and that's not awesome.

In addition, it might occur to you that none of these strategies are going to fix anything and you really don't have time for this nonsense. The good news is that you're half right. They're unlikely to fix anything, which is totally fine because You. Don't. Need. To. Be. Fixed.

You need kindness and compassion and forgiveness and a few minutes to relax and breathe and tend to your wounds, the wounds that life inevitably afflicts on every single one of us. But you don't need to be fixed.

With regard to your second point—that you don't have time for this nonsense—first of all, this isn't nonsense and I'm offended you would even think as much. (JK, JK, totally not offended. I get it. I used to feel the same way about self-care. You'll get over it.) Anyway, back to your busy schedule. I don't doubt for one moment that you're overwhelmed by everything you need to do. I get that. I feel the same way. But the other truth is that we humans manage to make time for what's important to us, and this stuff matters. But I promise you that it's way to easier to deal with everything when we're not buried in second arrows or army-crawling through our days because we just don't have the energy to do any better. (And, bonus, the more we practice

Find your own self-care arrows, and please don't judge yourself for whatever they may be. I love untangling knots (actual knots in necklaces, balls of yarn, whatever); it calms me down like nothing else. It doesn't matter if it's scrapbooking, strumming the ukulele, staring at the sky, or hitting the highway with the music turned up loud. As long as you enjoy it, and it heals you, then go for it.

self-care, the easier and more naturally it will come to us, until it's just another language we're fluent in.)

So keep on noticing your "fix it" or "I'm not worth it" or "I don't have time for this" second-arrow thoughts, and choose one of the following arrows of kind self-care instead:

Sip. Grab yourself a cup of water, tea, coffee, or anything soothing. Try to resist the urge to throw it back on your way out the door or while you're refereeing your kids' latest fight. That may be great for basic hydration, but it's not the vibe we're going for here. If you can, make your drink, take a seat, and ignore your kids for a minute while you sip and enjoy. One important note: This is not the time for alcohol. I'm not anti-drinking, but drinking isn't self-care. Alcohol is often a third-arrow avoidant behavior. It's a central nervous system depressant, and even though it might take the edge off your second-arrow thoughts for a few minutes, it also messes with your sleep and increases depression and anxiety over time. So enjoy a drink when it works for you, but please don't confuse it for self-care.

Snack. Take a moment and tune in to your body. When was the last time you ate? Are you hungry? Feeding ourselves is one of the kindest things we can do for ourselves. But for the vast majority of human beings, it's gotten completely tangled up in body image and rigid rules and judgment and shame and regret—and not because we're too weak or broken, but because we live in a society that makes it nearly impossible to have a healthy relationship with food.

Nourishing yourself in difficult moments isn't the same as eating your feelings. The former is about noticing your feelings of hunger or desire, honoring them, and giving yourself what you want in a kind and attentive way. The latter is about using food as a way to ignore, suppress, or deny your feelings. It's the difference between taking the time to figure out what you need and allowing yourself to slow down and enjoy it and scrounging for brownies before shoving a whole tray in your mouth. Untangling this stuff is *hard hard hard* for almost everyone, so if this feels too confusing or overwhelming to tackle right now, that's OK. You don't have to deal with this right now; there are a bunch of other ways to treat yourself with kindness in difficult moments. Pick one of those.

Stretch/soak. Our bodies absorb and carry the stress, anxiety, fear, anger, confusion, and overwhelm of our history, our present lives, and our worries about the future—whether we realize it or not. Our upset stomachs and tight-ass shoulders and backs that seem to go out every December for some strange reason generally don't come out of nowhere. And when we do take the time to notice what's happening AND take it seriously AND decide to respond in some way, we almost always focus on fixing it. We start some new-fangled diet or try some new stretching routine or go back to physical therapy. And all of that is great (well, maybe except the new-fangled diet bit), but they're not the same as kindness. And one of the kindest ways to respond to difficult moments, painful conflicts, or unpleasant feelings is by being nice to our bodies. (Which, I feel compelled to say again, isn't the same thing as improving them.)

So, take a moment to notice what you're feeling in your body and see if you can figure out what would feel good. Do you want to go for a walk or sit on your stoop and feel the sunshine on your face for a few minutes or take a nice long bath or go get yourself a massage? And if you can't do that for yourself right now, can you find another way to work a little body love into your day?

Snuggle. Physical touch is a powerful act of kindness for many people, and kids climbing all over you and coughing in your face and jamming their pointy-ass little elbows into your side DOES NOT COUNT. Even if you have a spouse or partner, there's no guarantee that you're getting the kind, connected touch you need: a hug, holding hands, snuggling, or, dare I say it, sex? If you need kind, connected touch, you may need to seek it out—perhaps by asking a friend for a hug, scheduling a date night with your partner, or even booking a damn hotel room if that's what it takes.

And if you don't have someone in your life who can provide this kind of touch, can you have compassion for yourself around that issue? This is about kindness, not adding to your list of things to feel like shit about.

And for those of you who already do have people in your lives who want / expect / need a lot of physical touch, let's just acknowledge that sometimes all this touching can feel like just one more thing you have to make time for or put on your endless to-do list. And that's when it's totally OK to ask for some space. Or every night until your kids are old enough to sleep past dawn.

Song or show. Sometimes we just need to dance or laugh or lose ourselves in the fantasy of another world, especially one that's about forty-seven minutes long and wraps up with the bad guy getting caught and the adorable couple ending up together and you get that warm fuzzy feeling like you swallowed a sweater but without having to go through the actual discomfort of swallowing said sweater.

Now, it can be super tricky to discern between the kindness of giving ourselves a freaking break and falling back into old third-arrow habits (which we all have—every single one of us—so don't beat yourself up about it). The trick, of course, is in the noticing. When we can step back and notice how we're feeling, what we're doing, how long we've been doing it for, and the fact that our streaming service actually has the audacity to ask us if we're still watching, well, that should give us the insight we need to figure out if we're treating ourselves with kindness or doing our damnedest to distract the hell out of ourselves.

Sleep. Sleep is such a hugely important deal that it gets its own box. When we're exhausted, we are at super high risk of all sorts of second- and third-arrow behaviors. Tired brains think all sorts of irrational, unhelpful thoughts, and not only do we think them, but we're far more likely to believe them. Making sleep a priority—whether that means saying no to nighttime meetings, going to bed early, or seeing a sleep consultant—is a powerful act of kindness. And when you can't get sleep for any reason (which happens to all of us, and is not your fault), that's just another opportunity to treat yourself with all kinds of compassion!

One final note about self-care. Please notice what's not on this list—social media. It can definitely be a source of connection (especially if you're connecting with supportive friends or community), but as anyone who's ever logged on to quickly check their messages only to end up a decade deep in their high-school nemesis's Instagram feed knows, your social media accounts can be a dangerous place to hang out. From bad news you really didn't need to hear to the latest posts from your practically perfect friend you can't help but compare yourself to, that screen is a landmine that you really don't want to trip over.

How Kindness Helps Our Kids

Each time we respond to our hardest moments with kindness, we're not only modeling that practice for our children, but we're also teaching them a number of powerful life lessons:

- Kindness isn't just something we do for other people.
- Every single one of us is worthy of kindness, even in our lowest, hardest, shittiest moments.
- Kindness isn't transactional. It's not tit for tat. It's not something we have to be good enough to deserve, or that we need to work for, or that we have to atone for later.
- Kindness isn't a weakness. It's fiercely empowering.
- Kindness isn't the same as being nice, and it's not about making ourselves or anyone else feel better.

When we take care of ourselves in very concrete ways (with the arrows of self-care, for example), we're not only teaching our children to do the same. We're also giving them permission to take care of themselves when they're suffering and to set boundaries when they need to. Finally, each time we treat our children with kindness, we're strengthening our relationship and giving them the opportunity to experience how healing, calming, and empowering compassion can be.

Advanced Kindness Practice: Loving Kindness Meditation

Most of us think of kindness as something we either do or don't do, but mostly lecture our children about. Just like connection and curiosity, though, kindness is a practice. It's something we can learn about (hence, this delightful chapter) and practice and get better at. And the better we get at it, the easier and more natural it becomes.

As I mentioned earlier, there are lots of different ways to be kind, and several of them are easy-ish to practice, including treating others with compassion. But the kindness of *self*-compassion is trickier because we're buried in first arrows (and possibly second and third arrows, depending on the situation) and we're freaking exhausted and stressed and anxious and pissed and not thinking clearly and the kids are whining and the dog pooped on the rug and fuuuuuck.

As anyone who's ever learned a second language knows, we almost always revert to our native language in stressful, painful, and scary moments. And for most of us, our native language is contempt.

So that sucks.

Fortunately, we can practice kindness, and not in the "random acts of kindness and senseless beauty" sort of way. Rather, we can practice kind self-talk, which is absolutely a gateway behavior for all of the rest of the kind self-care practices. And best of all, this practice doesn't require schlepping ourselves to a field across town at dinnertime, and no homework required. It's just taking the time to repeat a few simple phrases to ourselves.

These phrases come from the Buddhist practice of metta, or loving-kindness meditation. And no, you don't have to be a Buddhist or believe in anything specific to practice them. You just need to be willing to speak kindly to yourself. Here's how to do it:

1. Pick three or four phrases that you'll repeat. Here's what I use: May I be happy. May I be healthy. May I be safe. May I live with ease.

There are a lot of other options, so feel free to pick the ones that work for you. Options include:

- May I be free from danger.
- May I live safely.
- May I be mentally healthy.
- May I be physically healthy.
- May I be peaceful.
- May I be well.

- May my life be easy.
- May I find deep joy.
- May I be free of pain.
- May I be free from harm.
- May I be free of suffering.

These phrases will likely sound—and feel—super cheesy when you first start. Say them anyway. Finding and using your own words and phrases will help. You can use different words depending on what you need in a day, or you can stick with the same ones each time; whatever works for you. Remember, you're learning a new language. It takes time. Stick with it.

2. Find a few minutes—even just three or four if that's all you've got—and take a couple of deep breaths, just to settle and focus yourself. Sit in your car in the school parking lot for a few minutes after drop-off or before pick-up. Spend the first five minutes of your lunch break breathing and repeating.

3. Imagine someone who's always treated you with compassion and taken care of you. Someone kind and loving, with whom you have—or had—an easy and uncomplicated relationship. It could be a family member, a best friend, or your beloved cat. Send them some loving-kindness by thinking about them and saying your version of "May you be happy. May you be healthy. May you be safe. May you live with ease."

4. After you've repeated those phrases a few times, call to mind a neutral person. This could be your letter carrier or the bagger at the grocery store or the crossing guard outside your kids' school. Send them some loving-kindness by thinking about them and saying your version of "May you be happy. May you be healthy. May you be safe. May you live with ease."

5. Now think of someone who's driving you nuts. It could be that cousin who's always been a total jerk to you or your colleague who drives you batshit crazy or even your child. Don't start with the person you hate the most in the world or the one who brings you to your knees every time you see them. This is a practice. Start out slow. Take it easy. Send them some loving-kindness by thinking about them and saying your version of "May you be happy. May you be healthy. May you be safe. May you live with ease."

6. Once you're ready, turn your attention to yourself. Take a few deep breaths if you need to. Tell yourself, "May I be happy. May I be healthy. May I be safe. May I live with ease."

7. Take a few deep breaths, and let those words settle into your body. Rinse and repeat.

There's no right or wrong way to practice loving-kindness. Whether you spend two minutes sending loving-kindness to your pet ferret because they're the only living creature you can actually muster any positive feelings for in this moment or you spend the whole time focused on yourself because damn you really need it right now, that's exactly the perfect way to practice.

The loving-kindness meditation traditionally starts with sending kind thoughts toward ourselves, and then on to beloved individuals (or pets), then neutral folks, challenging people, and finally, the whole world. As this meditation became more popular in the West, teachers realized that their students just found it too damn hard to start by sending loving-kindness to themselves. It was too awkward, too uncomfortable, too foreign. They just didn't think they were worthy. So meditation teachers modified the practice, letting folks start by focusing on people they love and building their way up to themselves.

The first time I heard that story, I nearly burst into tears. (OK, fine, I'm a crier. What can I say?) But seriously. How sad is that? How sad is it that so many of us didn't even think we were worthy of wishing ourselves the most basic human rights: happiness, health, safety, and ease? If that feels true for you, please don't feel bad about it or beat yourself up for it. Just try to have a whole lot of compassion for yourself and keep practicing.

The Most Important Thing to Remember: Kindness is the antidote to contempt. You are always, always worthy of kindness. No. Matter. What.

CHAPTER EIGHT

How to Compassion the Crap Out of Your Kids

It was a warm Sunday, not long after the start of school last fall. Our eleven-year-old daughter was eager to hang out with a new kid in her class, and he lived across the street from a big park where they could play. We were already a year into the pandemic, and we were desperate for safe social interactions. This one was a no-brainer.

She came home hours later, pink-cheeked and happy. It wasn't until after dinner that night that I got all the details, including the part where my kiddo and her friend walked over a mile to get ice cream. At first, I was pleased by their initiative and independence, but as I thought about it more, I realized that the ice cream shop they went to had no outdoor seating. Our family wasn't eating inside restaurants during the pandemic—I mean like *at all*—so I was a bit confused. Did they just stand on the sidewalk?

"So, where did you guys eat your ice cream?"

My daughter paused, and in that second, my heart sank.

"Inside," she said. "We sat in a booth." Another pause. "But it was only for like, two minutes. And we were in the corner."

Holy shit.

My whole body tensed up and my thoughts exploded. We had worked so hard to give our kids as much independence and autonomy and opportunities to hang out with their friends as we could during this freaking pandemic, and we tried hard not to burden them with rules and restrictions. But eating in restaurants was a hard no, and she knew it.

She knew it, and she did it anyway.

And I knew, from lots and lots of experience, that my own freak-out was imminent. I was about to lose my shit with her. And I could have, honestly. A parental explosion would have been completely justified in that moment. She had broken a core pandemic rule that could potentially put the whole family's health at risk. So, yeah, I could have reacted all shouty-style and laid the smack down—no more unchaperoned hangouts and no more ice cream until she goes to college. (Which, for the record, would have been a terrible idea for the whole family. Not only did my husband and I need the time away from our daughters as much as they needed it from us, but god help me if you think I can make it through the rest of my daughters' middle school and high school years without ice cream.)

Even so, I thought about it. Boy, did I think about it. I could have yelled all my tension out AND taught my kid a lesson she wouldn't ever forget AND reasserted my authority in a time when everything felt so damn out of control. It was an awfully tempting possibility, to be honest.

But I didn't do it. Maybe it's because I was working on this book and the hypocrisy of it all was too much to handle. Or maybe it was because I took one look at my daughter's pained face and saw that she already knew, like deep down in her kishkes knew, that she had screwed up big time. Or maybe it's because I know—after years of experience and experimenting—that freaking out never works out. The kid doesn't learn the skills they need to do better next time; they just learn how to get better at hiding their mistakes and poor life choices from their parents. And that's not what I want, especially as my daughters head into their teen years. I want them to keep talking to me, even and especially when they've epically screwed up.

I took a deep breath. A really, really deep breath.

"Alright, kiddo, here's the deal," I said. "We're both too tired to deal with this right now. Let's both get some sleep and we can talk about it tomorrow. Meanwhile, I love you, no matter what."

I won't lie; I felt pretty damn proud of myself for keeping my cool in that moment.

And then I did what any reasonable parent would do. I went downstairs and unloaded on my husband.

It's been over a year since any of us have eaten in a restaurant and we're working so hard to keep her grandparents safe and what the hell was she thinking and BLAH BLAH BLAH GAAAAHHHHHHH.

I did feel a teensy bit better after that.

We didn't have time to talk until dinner the next night, which was good, because I legitimately needed that entire day to get calm enough and clear enough to think through how I wanted to approach things. I decided to start with curiosity, if for no other reason than I could not even begin to fathom *why* my kiddo had eaten her ice cream inside. And so that was my first question.

Not surprisingly, as we'll discuss later in this chapter, "why" questions don't tend to be very effective, and mine was no exception. All I got was a mumbled "I don't know" in response. And here's the thing: I believed her. For some reason, in that moment, I totally believed that my daughter did not, in fact, know why she had eaten her ice cream in the restaurant.

So I tried a different tactic.

In as calm a voice as I could muster, I said, "Try to remember back to when you and your friend were getting your ice cream. What were you thinking about?"

She was quiet for a moment and then she said, "I was thinking about ice cream."

And that absolutely made sense to me. My kiddo is generally respectful and usually either a) follows the rules, or b) talks to us about why they don't make sense to her. And she's just a kid with a kid's brain, which means she can easily get caught up in the momentum of the moment and forget about anything other than whatever's right in front of her, especially when the thing right in front of her is an ice cream cone.

From that place of shared understanding, we were able to have a conversation about what made it hard to remember the family pandemic rules. My daughter cried as she talked about how challenging it had been, not being able to hang out with her friends inside and eat inside and do freaking normal-ass activities (my words on that last one, not hers) for so long, and I totally understood that. I had been feeling it too. It had been rough for all of us, and all she wanted was to enjoy a treat in a restaurant. And that's when I went in with the kindness: I took her onto my lap and held her, and I may have even cried a bit myself.

Once we were both a little calmer, we talked about how to help her remember the rules the next time. She came up with a few ideas, such as having us talk to her friends' parents and reviewing the rules with her ahead of time.

After all that, we didn't take away the hangouts or the ice cream or even her screen time. Our daughter understood what she had done wrong, she felt terrible about it, and we had a plan for how she would do things differently next time. But let me very clear: At no point did we ever tell her that what she had done wasn't a big deal, or that it was OK if she did it again, or that we would consider flexing our family rules because she wanted to eat ice cream inside. We held firm to our expectations and made it clear that if she couldn't follow them, then she would likely need a parent to join her when she hung out with friends—not as a punishment, but as an acknowledgment that she wasn't ready to make these sorts of decisions on her own yet.

That's the magic of compassion: It decreases stress and tension, which allows us to get a little clarity on the situation, so we can solve problems and plan for the future without flexing our rules and boundaries, giving in to our kids, or letting them get away with anything. And compassion does all of this while opening up communication and strengthening our relationship with our kids. Oh, and it feels better for everyone. It's a win-win-win, which, as I'm sure I don't need to tell you, doesn't happen very often in the world of parenting, so we gotta jump on it when we can.

If Compassioning the Crap Out of Our Kids Is So Awesome, Why Don't We Do It All the Time?

I'm writing this chapter a few months after the Infamous Ice Cream Incident, and as I reflect on it, compassion seems like such the obvious choice. And yet it took me years of losing my shit and laying the smack down to get there. I know I'm not alone; the default reaction for most parents is to freak out and/or focus on finding fault.

But why? If compassion is so effective at reducing stress, changing behaviors, and strengthening relationships, why aren't we all just compassioning the crap out of our kids all the time? There are a bunch of reasons, and none of them have to do with you or your inherent worth as a person, much less your parenting skills or abilities.

We didn't know any better. It's not just that we didn't grow up speaking the language of self-compassion; it's that we didn't even know the language *existed.* (And for the record, neither did our parents. Or their parents.) That's not to say no one in the history of the universe ever treated themselves with compassion. Of course not. It's just that the idea that compassion is a skill that we could intentionally practice hadn't yet made its way into the Western mindset. This stuff is new for all of us.

Most of us were raised in a culture that believes we need to discipline our children in order to maintain respect and control. We've been taught that either we lay the smack down and show our kids who's boss or all hell will break loose. We've been told, by our parents and parenting experts and social media mavens, that chaos isn't the normal, predictable outcome of life with kids. Rather it's because we're not parenting hard enough or well enough or we don't have our shit together.

Yeah, that's a load of crap.

Control is, as they say, an illusion—especially when it comes to kids. And the older our kids get, the less control we have over them. Eventually, the only thing that's going to keep them connected to us is the quality of our relationship with them, which isn't likely to be very strong if we've spent years screaming at them and taking away their screens every time they screw up.

We're too damn tired and overwhelmed and burned out to show up for our kids with compassion. This isn't a matter of willpower or inner strength or whatever. It's how our brains work when the shit hits the fan. Tired parent brain = toddler running the show. (And oh, what a terrible, terrible show it is.) Well-rested parent brain = the grown-up is back in charge and can choose to take a deep breath and respond with compassion.

Here's the thing about exhaustion: It's not just about how much sleep we get (or don't). There are so many ways to be depleted—physical fatigue, mental, emotional, social, spiritual, sensory, creative, the list goes on and on—and most parents are drained in every single one of them. Sometimes there's something we can do about some of them, and oftentimes, there's no easy or clear fix. Sometimes all we can do is muster enough energy to turn on an episode of *PAW Patrol* or *MasterChef Junior* so we can zone out on the couch. Even that can be a deeply compassionate response for the entire family.

Good enough parenting is absolutely good enough. It would be great if we could respond to our children with perfectly calibrated compassion at every moment, but that ain't gonna happen. Perfection isn't an option, and even if it were, it's not ideal for our kids. Children benefit tremendously from our mistakes and missteps, and not just because they're learning what not to do. Each time we forget to sign their permission slip or lecture when we should be listening or send them to their rooms when we should be pulling them onto our laps, we're teaching our kids some of life's best lessons:

- They will not always get what they want—or even need—and *they will be OK.*
- We all make mistakes and we can always apologize and make things right again.
- People can have strong and unpleasant emotions all over us and say the wrong things and do the wrong things and that doesn't mean that we're terrible people or they hate us or our relationship sucks. It just means that we're all human and this is what humans do—especially to people they love.
- We can notice when we've gotten off course and choose to treat ourselves and others with compassion at any moment.

What to Do Instead: How to Compassion the Crap Out of Your Kids

Our kids will struggle and suffer for the rest of their lives. That's the bad news, and nothing to blame yourself for. It's just life. The good news is that we parents now have a more skillful option for responding to them. While compassion can take some getting used to, it's way, way more effective than losing our shit or lecturing them or just zoning out and letting them suffer alone because we're too overwhelmed and have no freaking clue how to help our kids. Remembering these two acronyms can help you get started: KISS and SNACKS.

KISS: Keep It Simple, Sugar

Please please don't make this bigger than it needs to be. Try not to overthink it or get all worked up about it or hyper-focused on saying the perfect thing at just the right time. You're not their therapist and it's not your job to solve the problem or fix their feelings or make everything perfect and better. That sort of response is neither necessary nor possible, so do what you can to let those fantasies go. Just **Keep It Simple, Sugar**. It's just about showing up, sticking around, and mustering as much connection, curiosity, and kindness as we can when the chaos really ramps up. That's all our kids really need.

SNACKS: Stop, Notice, Accept, Connect, Get Curious, Kill Them with Kindness, and Start Again

Sometimes it's hard to know how to be compassionate with our children. It's so tempting to focus on fixing the problem or their feelings or whatever, but that's not what compassion is all about. Instead, try showing up with SNACKS (because honestly, what kid doesn't love a snack?).

STEP 1: STOP

We can't show up for our kids when we're doing something else. It's just not possible. But it's not always easy to put a pin in whatever we're doing, because generally speaking, whatever we're doing likely feels either a) way more urgent, or b) way more entertaining than whatever our child is struggling with. It can be legitimately hard to step away from our work or our friends or the screen or whatever else is holding our attention and focus on our kids, but that's OK. You're not stopping forever, just for a moment. And no matter how hard it feels, we can do hard things, and they will get easier with practice.

STEP 2: NOTICE

You're probably thinking that this is the dumbest piece of advice ever because of course you freaking notice when your kid is suffering and struggling. You notice the hell out of their tantrums and fighting and door slamming. You couldn't freaking miss it if you tried, and more often than not, you're consumed by it.

Yeah. That's not noticing.

Noticing is the difference between biting your toddler's head off because he's being a total pain in your ass and getting just enough headspace to realize that you forgot about lunch and he just needs a little food to get back on track.

Noticing is the difference between getting into yet another epic power struggle with your tween about her clothing choices and choosing to step out of the room, take a few deep breaths, and figure out if this is really the hill you want to die on. (PS: It's probably not.)

Noticing is the difference between screaming at your kids to stop freaking bickering already and remembering that sometimes it's OK to let kids figure things out for themselves.

Noticing is the difference between holding yourself responsible for your child's feelings and getting enough clarity to remind yourself that a) no feeling is ever wrong, b) feelings were meant to be felt, not fixed, and c) it's absolutely not your job to make your kiddo feel better. All you need to do is stick with them through the storm.

Sometimes it's hard to know what to do with what we notice, especially if what we notice is really weird or scary or confusing. Do we worry? (OK, obviously we worry, so the question is really what level of worry are we talking about here?) If you're not sure, check in with trusted friends or adults who know you and your children, which may include friends, family members, teachers, their pediatrician, or their therapist. Remember, you don't ever have to be scared alone.

STEP 3: ACCEPT

This one's a doozy, but it's well worth the time and effort. There is zero space for compassion, connection, curiosity, and kindness if we're all tangled up in wishing our kids were different or being pissed at their imperfections or refusing to acknowledge whatever they're struggling with. All of these reactions are completely natural, and we all have them, but that doesn't mean they're helpful. So give yourself a little time to feel your feelings or vent to your partner or sob with your therapist or whatever you need to do—because we all need to do that—and have a shitload of compassion for yourself because man this parenting gig is HARD AF. And then accept that this is where your kids are right now, and this is what they're struggling with. Again, that doesn't mean you like it, and it doesn't mean you aren't going to work with your kids to change it. It just means it is what it is right now. That's all.

STEP 4: CONNECT

"Connection before redirection" is a favorite saying among parenting experts, and not just because we love us a good rhyme. It's also because lecturing or explaining or setting limits or laying the smack down will get you nowhere unless you've taken the time to connect first. This is true for our children, our partners, our colleagues, or anyone else in our lives. Think back to the last time someone barged in when you were having a rough moment and started in on everything you did wrong and everything you should have done differently (or even worse, told you to just calm down), without taking even a moment to say hi, ask how you were doing, or understand what was going on for you? How did that go for you? Did you feel any calmer? Clearer? Inspired to change?

Those were rhetorical questions. Of course you didn't.

Connection makes all the difference. It's the most effective and efficient way to help everyone calm down and move forward with clarity, creativity, and confidence. But you can't bullshit it, and you can't fake it. Kids have excellent BS detectors and they'll know when you're phoning it in. They may not realize what they know, and they might not be able to verbalize what they know, but on some deep level, they'll know it and you'll know it and it will not feel awesome.

And just as you can't fake connection, you also can't force it. Snuggling a frustrated toddler who doesn't want to be touched or repeatedly nagging an exasperated tween to talk to you isn't connecting. They're just fix or feel-better reactions, designed to soothe our own anxiety and discomfort about whatever's going on with our kids. It's the grown-up (ish) version of "Please play with me will you play with me why won't you play with meeeeeee?" and it's as ineffective and annoying when you do it to your children as it is to you when they do it to you.

Here are a few connection strategies to try instead:

Play It Cool and Keep It Casual. It can be tempting to get all serious and show up in a super serious way or have a serious conversation, but that's not necessary. The whole talking face-to-face thing is overrated anyway, especially when it comes to kids (and that's coming from a woman who made her career talking to people face-to-face). Eye contact can make things unnecessarily intense and increase stress. So try something else. Some kids connect physically, through snuggling or wrestling, while others might want to be near you without touching. Some kiddos like to talk, while others find it easier to connect through a shared activity, like coloring or crafting, going for a walk, shooting hoops, or tossing a ball. Remember, this isn't about what you need, at least not in this moment. It's about noticing and accepting what your kid needs in that moment.

Name and acknowledge your child's feelings if you can. Daniel Siegel, my favorite interpersonal neurobiologist (because we all have one of those, don't we?), frequently reminds us to "name it to tame it," and by *it*, he means our feelings. There's something magical about acknowledging what we're feeling, and it can be a great way to connect with a struggling child. Having said that, resist the urge to start your sentences with "I know you're feeling . . ." That can feel bossy and judgy and put your kid on the defensive. Try something like, "I'm wondering if that made you feel sad . . ." or "It sounds like maybe you're feeling . . ." Feel free to use your own words and style, and for the love of god try not to sound all therapist-y; that's annoying.

Don't tell your child that he or she is OK. Clearly they're not OK; otherwise you wouldn't be KISSing and SNACKing them. You can tell them that they're safe, or that they will be OK, or that this feeling won't last forever.

Let them know that they're not the only ones who have been through this situation. Offer to share a story about a time when you went through something similar, if you have one. This doesn't have to be a story about how you handled everything perfectly and it all came out perfectly; it might even be better if it isn't. The point is that you got through it, and your kid will too.

Remember that it's OK to set limits on behaviors and make the distinction between behavior and feelings. Your kids can be rip-shit pissed; they can't whack their brother over the head with a whiffle ball bat or dump an entire bowl of peas on the floor.

For older kids, tweens, and teens: Ask them if they're looking for advice or just someone to listen and *respect their response.* If they don't want advice, I don't care if you have the best solution ever in the history of life solutions that will 100 percent solve their problem for all eternity (which, PS, you don't), bite your tongue and zip your trap and keep it to yourself.

STEP 5: GET CURIOUS

Curiosity is a parental superpower (when we can remember to use it). Not only is it a great way to connect with our kids and figure out what the hell is going on, but it's pretty much the only way to share information with our kids without sounding preachy. We've already talked about how folks feel about unsolicited advice, and there's no one who likes it less than a kid getting it from their parents. Just telling your kids that feelings are normal, and each feeling has a beginning, middle, or end, for example, is likely to land on deaf, uninterested ears. (Trust me, I know from experience. Lots and lots of experience.) But asking kids where they are in their feelings—the beginning, middle, or end—will have a much higher probability of sparking their interest. Each time we can ask a question or preface our thoughts with words like "I wonder what would happen if . . ." we're welcoming our children into the conversation rather than throwing it in their faces.

You really can't go wrong with curiosity, but there are a few strategies that will help make your curiosity practice as effective and engaging as possible.

Turn on your own curiosity first. Here are a few questions that might be useful to consider:

- What's going on with them? What are they struggling with? Developmental transitions? Something at school? With their siblings or friends? Their teams or extracurricular activities?
- Are they dealing with any major life changes? Starting or ending the school year? Transitioning to preschool, elementary school, or middle school? Going to camp for the first time? Any birthdays, holidays, or significant anniversaries coming up?
- What's your best guess at how they might be feeling? Do you think they're dealing with any big, overwhelming, or frightening emotions? Are they worried about or scared of something?
- Have they been dealing with any losses in the past few months? A grandparent? A pet? A divorce in the family? A best friend who moved away?

- What's going on with their bodies? Are they in the middle of a growth spurt? Could they be in pain? Starting puberty? Could they be hungry, thirsty, tired, getting sick, or constipated?

- What do they need? (Try not to confuse this with what they're saying they need; they're just kids with poorly developed prefrontal cortexes, so they might not actually know what they need. Try not to get too frustrated; as annoying as this can be, it's totally normal.)

- Can you give them what they need? And if you can, does that mean you should? And if you can't or don't want to, what can you do instead?

Try to avoid "why" questions. "Why did you do that?" is a parental favorite, which is weird, because it rarely works. Kids (and adults too!) often don't have the insight or information to answer that question accurately or honestly, so either they'll shut down with an "I don't know," or they'll make up a story that may be neither accurate nor helpful. You can often get the answer you're looking for with questions such as:

- What were you doing when that happened?
- What did you want at the time?
- How are you feeling?
- Do you remember what you were thinking about?
- What do you think that was about?

Try to notice if you're expecting a specific response from your child. That's not curiosity; that's a quiz. If you notice that you're feeling judgmental, annoyed, or irritated at whatever your kid is showing up with, then you're probably not in a headspace to be curious, and that's OK. Go back to connection or kindness or tag in your parenting partner or put the kid in front of the TV until you've had a cup of tea or a few minutes to breathe. Any of that will be more effective than judging your children for their answer.

Ditch the snarky, sarcastic questions. Unless you are 100 percent absolutely positively certain that you and your kids are calm and connected and ready for a dose of humor. Otherwise, those kinds of questions are just going to alienate your kiddo, possibly hurt their feelings, and shatter any chance you might have had at connection and compassion in that moment.

Your child might not always be interested in, or receptive to, your curiosity.

That's OK. Sometimes kids just don't feel like exploring or thinking or talking or insighting (which is different from inciting, and really should be a word), and I know you know what I'm talking about because that's how almost every parent on the planet feels after about six p.m. And that's cool, because you can still kill them with kindness.

STEP 6: KILL THEM WITH KINDNESS

Kindness is awesome. It's at the heart of connection and curiosity, and it's always an option, as long as you can get in the head- and heart-space for it. But please don't misunderstand me; we're not going for a Mother Teresa level of kindness here. (And, for the record, Mother Teresa didn't actually have kids. I'm just sayin'.) I mean, if you've got next-level kindness skills, that's awesome, but most of us don't. We're just aiming for enough kindness to not beat up ourselves or our kids for whatever normal, but brutal, human situation we're dealing with.

All you need to do is reach into your quiver of kindness arrows, pull out whichever one feels right in the moment, and do it *with* your child. There's no perfect practice here, so don't stress about that. Each one of these is inherently kind and can often set the stage for connection and curiosity as well.

Here is a not-at-all exhaustive list to get you started, in no particular order:

Snack 'n' Sip (as in an actual snack, not a clever acronym made up by that awesome parenting lady). I'm not suggesting you teach your children to eat or drink their feelings, but noticing and tending to our bodies' needs is an inherently kind thing to do—especially when you can share that snack together.

Stretch. Move your bodies. Have a kitchen dance party. Go for a walk. Sit on the floor and stretch together. Not only is this a great way to connect, but it often feels good as well. And don't forget, our feelings live in our bodies, and, man, can they get stuck there.

Stretching and moving can help loosen up those feelings, which will take away some of their power.

Snuggle. Because snuggling is awesome.

Song. Turn on some tunes, and either dance or just listen. Music is a great way to evoke and acknowledge emotions, and sometimes you gotta just get those feelings out.

Story. There are so many ways this one can go. You can share a story from your own life, make up a story together, or read a book. Books are often great choices because a) they require relatively little brain power from weary parents, and b) they can be a highly effective way to explore confusing situations and big feelings when we have no idea where to start or what to say. Don't worry about finding the perfect book; just take your kiddo to the library and let them pick whatever they want. You'll be amazed at how often they pick a story that's just right for whatever's going on.

Show. Turn on something you both like and watch *together*. Bonus points for snuggling (if that works for you and your kid).

Sleep. Our kids don't appreciate this now, but sleep is an inherently kind way to take care of our minds and bodies. Tired brains think too much, feel too big, and get all worked up when really the only problem is that they're exhausted. I'll often tell my worn-out, freaking-out daughter "We're too tired to talk about this now. Get some sleep, and if this is still on your mind in the morning, we'll handle it." Nine times out of ten, we don't end up talking about it at all. (One important note: If I think it's a thing we should talk about—like the Ice Cream Incident—we'll abso-freaking-lutely talk about it the next day.)

I want you to notice one thing that's not on this list: solo screentime. Watching a show with your kiddo is a completely different experience from sticking them in front of a screen alone. Don't get me wrong; screentime for kids can be a very kind thing for parents to do for themselves, especially if it's in the middle of, I don't know, a freaking pandemic and you haven't had a moment to yourself since March 2020. That's 100 percent legit. But if you're going for compassion toward your children, letting them zombie out in front of a screen alone ain't on the list. I'm not suggesting that you never hand them the tablet; I'm just wanting you to know the difference so you can make the most skillful decision at any given moment.

STEP 7: START AGAIN.

We can always, always start again. Modeling that for our children and creating the space for them to start again is one of the great gifts we can give them.

KISS and SNACKS. Those are the core practices for compassioning the crap out of your kids. And you can do all of these things—every single one of them—while also holding your boundaries, rules, and expectations. I have held my daughter in my lap as she sobbed about not getting the cookie she really freaking wanted even as I continued to say no to said cookie, and you can too. It might not always feel good, and it will probably require you to tolerate your child's unhappiness rather than immediately soothing it away, but it will strengthen your relationship with them and teach them the skills, strategies, confidence, and resilience to tackle any challenges they face in life.

One Final Super Important Note About Compassioning the Crap Out Your Kids

In Chapter 7, I said that we don't practice self-compassion so we can feel better. We treat ourselves with compassion because we feel bad. It's a subtle but SUPER important distinction that's worth remembering when you're compassioning the crap out of your kids. You're not doing it to make them feel better, because, as crazy as it may sound, it's not your job to make your kids feel better.

Let's say it one more time together.

It's not your job to make your kids feel better.

Every time we parents get all caught up in how our children feel and trying to make them feel happier, we're setting ourselves up for a whole lotta problems. As anyone who has ever tried to get a newborn to sleep through the night or a toddler to poop on the potty or a teenager to, I don't know, DO ANYTHING AT ALL, trying to control something that is absolutely uncontrollable will wear you down and stress you out faster than a fifth grader with a science project due in the morning. There are very few ways to make yourself crazier faster than trying to fix someone else's feelings, especially when that someone else happens to be your own child who likely has very strong feelings that they express loudly and inappropriately and all over you, which, if you're not careful, is likely to elicit very strong feelings in you that you will also very likely express inappropriately all over your kids.

Your job is to notice when your child is suffering and connect with them with curiosity and kindness. They might end up feeling better; they might not. While I'm definitely on Team Feel Better, that's not your job, and as long as you're showing up for your kids, everyone wins.

Advanced Compassioning the Crap Out of Your Kids Practice: When You're Pissed, Try Loving Kindness Instead

You will get pissed at your kids. I don't care if you just spent a week eating kale and drinking kombucha at a loving-kindness retreat; something will happen and you will feel angry at your children. Fortunately for you, you've read this book and you know now that no feeling is ever wrong, so you're not beating yourself up for feeling angry. And instead of getting swept up in your anger, you're going to notice it and have a whole lot of compassion for yourself in this rough time.

That might be enough to calm you down, but depending on the temperature of your rage and whether or not you've slept in the last week (because we all know you didn't actually go on that kale and kombucha retreat), it might not be. You might still feel like throttling that little punk. And that's when you can send a little loving-kindness their way.

Just take a deep breath, picture your children in a happier moment, and remember your phrases:

May you be happy.

May you be healthy.

May you be safe.

May you live with ease.

May you not be on the receiving end of my epic shit-loss.

Now let me be very clear. This is 100 percent fake it until you make it. That's totally OK. You will make it. Repeat it until you believe it. Or at least until you're feeling a whole lot calmer and clearer.

The Most Important Thing to Remember: It's not your job to make your children feel better. It's your job to notice when they're suffering and respond with compassion.

CHAPTER NINE

A Recap of Key Points and How to Make the Magic Happen

Woo-hoo! You made it to the end of a parenting book! Or you knew enough to skip to the summary chapter! Either way, well done, you.

Over the past eight chapters, we went through a HUGE amount of information, during which time I basically asked you to completely rejigger your entire way of thinking about your life and parenting.

It's a lot. I get it. I get it because I've been there and some days I'm still there. And I promise I wouldn't lay this on you if it wasn't important. As in, big-time, majorly life-changing important.

Fortunately, compassion isn't complicated. And the more you practice it, the easier and more natural it will become, and the easier and more fun your life and parenting will be, which is awesome. And whenever you forget to treat yourself with compassion and kindness, that's just another opportunity for you to compassion the crap out of yourself . . . for not practicing your compassion. Sounds crazy, but it actually makes sense when you think about it.

But don't think too hard about it. Seriously. One of the dynamics I've seen time and again in hurried, harried parents (myself included) is that we get all tangled up in the details of getting our latest program or plan just perfectly right, and then if we don't absolutely nail it, we give up. That's bananas. That's like pulling your kids out of school if they don't get an A+ on every single homework assignment and exam. And I know you wouldn't do that because then your kids would be home with you all day long. Oh, and also because it's BONKERBALLS.

Instead, just remind yourself, over and over again, that you can always go back to compassion—for yourself, and your children.

The Most Important Points

Here's a quick review of the most important points of the book and how to put them into practice.

- Shitty Parent Syndrome is the thought, belief, or perception that you're a shitty parent, and that belief leaves us feeling confused and insecure about how to raise our children.
- The first arrows of life are painful, but they're unavoidable. The second arrows of suffering and the third arrows of denial and distraction are completely normal human reactions to our suffering, but they also make life and parenting harder and less fun. Unlike first arrows, these are optional.
- Chaos is the normal, predictable outcome of life with kids. It doesn't necessarily mean we're not parenting well enough or doing anything wrong.
- Far too often in parenting we're stuck choosing between bad and worse, and we have no idea which option is bad and which one is worse. All we can do is make our best guess and have a shitload of compassion for ourselves in the process.

- Compassion is the practice of responding to suffering with connection, curiosity, and kindness instead of isolation, judgment, and self-contempt.

- Self-compassion isn't self-pity, self-indulgence, self-esteem, self-improvement, or letting yourself off the hook. Self-compassion is an incredibly powerful and effective way to respond to the shitty first arrows of life.

- Self-compassion is a practice, and the more you do it, the easier and more naturally it will come to you.

- When we get stressed and don't know how to respond to situations, we often freak out: fight, flight, freeze, flip out, fix, or fawn.

- The more we practice self-compassion, the more we can manage our lives and parent our children from a place of calm clarity, creativity, and confidence.

- We don't practice self-compassion to make ourselves better. Each time we focus on making ourselves feel better, the underlying message we're sending ourselves is that it's not OK to feel bad. But it's OK to feel like crap. We treat ourselves with compassion *because* we feel bad, and our suffering—all suffering—is worthy of kindness. It's OK to not feel better. It's OK to feel bad and take care of ourselves in the process.

- Noticing, or the ability to be aware of the chaos in our own brains and lives without getting swept away by it, is the first and necessary step in the practice of self-compassion.

- Connection is the antidote to shame. Remembering that parenting is incredibly hard for every single one of us and connecting with the people who love us and will be real with us as often as possible are game changers.
- Curiosity, or the ability to get interested in whatever's going on in our lives—and take our responses seriously—is the antidote to judgment. It calms us down and helps us get clarity about whatever is going on.
- Kindness calls on us to treat ourselves with respect rather than contempt, set aside the need to fix ourselves, and respond to our suffering with the arrows of kind self-care.
- Compassioning the crap out of your kids is a highly effective way to resolve difficult situations and respond to your children's hardest moments while also strengthening your relationship and teaching them valuable skills for the future.

Seven Acronyms to Kick-Start Your Self-Compassion Practice

Acronyms are one of my favorite ways to remember an idea or practice without getting all bogged down in the details, which is why I've scattered them throughout this book like glitter. I've gathered all of the acronyms from the book here, and hopefully they'll remind you to put down your second arrow and treat yourself with compassion each time the shit hits the fan.

SNAFU: Shit happens to all of us. No matter how personal it may feel, it's just another SNAFU. Situation Normal, All Fucked Up. Normal. It happens to all of us.

CHAOS: Chaos is just part of the deal, and Compassion Helps Alleviate Our Suffering.

STOP: Noticing our own suffering is the first step toward treating ourselves with compassion. All you need to do is Stop, Take a Breath, Observe, and Proceed.

HALT: If you're having a hard time figuring out how you feel or what you need, ask yourself if you're Hungry, Angry, Lonely, or Tired.

CALM: Your body is an important source of information about how you're doing. Checking in with your Chest, Arms, Legs, and Mind is a great way to get curious about your body.

KISS: Keep It Simple, Sugar. Don't make this more complicated than it needs to be. You got this.

SNACKS: Every time you're suffering or struggling, reach for your SNACKS.

Stop what you're doing,

Notice what's going on,

Accept it (rather than fight with it),

Connect with common humanity and/or real actual people,

Get Curious about your experience, and

Be super Kind to yourself.

Oh, and remember you can always, always, Start Again.

Some Awesome Books That Will Help You Have More Compassion for Yourself and Your Kids

There are a ton of different ways to talk about, think about, and practice self-compassion, and finding a book or teacher or podcast that aligns with your style and preferences is a great place to start. In this section, I've listed a variety of self-compassion and parenting books that offer excellent advice and (hopefully) do it in a way that won't amp up your shame or self-doubt. Having said that, if you find yourself reading one of these books—or any book, for that matter—that triggers your second-arrow thinking, DITCH IT. Ditch it immediately. Do not pass go, do not collect $200 (unless you can actually collect $200, in which case, grab the cash and ditch the book). The point here is that the problem is the book, not you.

Self-Compassion

The Difficult Thing of Being Human: The Art of Self-Compassion by Bodhipaksa (Parallax Press, 2019)

How to Be Nice to Yourself: The Everyday Guide to Self-Compassion by Laura Silberstein-Tirch (Althea Press, 2019)

The Mindful Path to Self-Compassion: Freeing Yourself from Destructive Thoughts and Emotions by Christopher Germer (Guilford Publications, 2009)

Real Love: The Art of Mindful Connection by Sharon Salzberg (Flatiron Books, 2017)

Self-Compassion for Parents: Nurture Your Child by Caring for Yourself by Susan Pollak (Guilford Publications, 2019)

Self-Compassion: The Proven Power of Being Kind to Yourself by Kristin Neff (HarperCollins, 2011)

Parenting

All Joy and No Fun: The Paradox of Modern Parenthood by Jennifer Senior (Ecco, 2014)

*How to Stop Losing Your Sh*t with Your Kids: A Practical Guide to Becoming a Calmer, Happier Parent* by Carla Naumburg (Workman Publishing, 2019)

Mindful Discipline: A Loving Approach to Setting Limits and Raising an Emotionally Intelligent Child by Shauna Shapiro and Chris White (New Harbinger Publications, 2014)

Raising Good Humans: A Mindful Guide to Breaking the Cycle of Reactive Parenting and Raising Kind, Confident Kids by Hunter Clarke-Fields (New Harbinger Publications, 2019)

Ready, Set, Breathe: Practicing Mindfulness with Your Children for Fewer Meltdowns and a More Peaceful Family by Carla Naumburg (New Harbinger Publications, 2015)

Strong as a Mother: How to Stay Healthy, Happy, and (Most Importantly) Sane from Pregnancy to Parenthood: The Only Guide to Taking Care of YOU! by Kate Rope (St. Martin's Griffin, 2018)

There Are Moms Way Worse Than You: Irrefutable Proof That You Are Indeed a Fantastic Parent by Glenn Boozan, illustrated by Priscilla Witte (Workman Publishing, 2022)

ACKNOWLEDGMENTS

This book wouldn't exist without the wise, hilarious guidance of my amazing agent, Gillian MacKenzie, and book coach extraordinaire, Jennie Nash. You two are the best.

So much gratitude to the entire Workman team: my amazing editor, Maisie Tivnan, and the rest of the crew, including Analucia Zepeda; the publicity powerhouse of Rebecca Carlisle, Ilana Gold, and Abigail Sokolsky; and the production and design wizards Doug Wolff, Barbara Peragine, Beth Levy, Sasha Tropp, and Sarah Smith. A special shout-out to the sensitivity reader, Ronica Davis, whose sharp eye and thoughtful perspective helped make my snarky voice as respectful and inclusive as possible.

I wrote this book during the craziest of days of the pandemic, and I never would have made it through without my crew, who made me laugh, kept me grounded, and always showed up with a shitload of compassion: Rachel Pytel, Kathleen Flinton, Abigail Gongora, Kate Rope, Liz Rudnick, my sister Daniela Silverstein, and the Library Squad: Mara Acel-Green, Ana Volpi, Rachel Fish, Nicole Gann, Jenny Gomeringer, and Deb Gaffin.

Finally, to my husband, Josh, and my girls, Frieda and Rose. You're my favorite humans, and I'm grateful for you every single day.

ABOUT THE AUTHOR

Carla Naumburg, PhD, is a clinical social worker, writer, and mother. She is the author of five books, including the bestselling *How to Stop Losing Your Sh*t with Your Kids*. Carla lives in Massachusetts with her husband and two daughters.